D1133181

# Pastry 2009

## in europe

# index

# Colofon

Pastry in Europe is an annual edition
of Culibooks Inc. bvba
Picardielaan 22, B-2970 Schilde – Belgium
phone  +32 33 80 17 00
fax  +32 33 80 17 10
www.PastryInEurope.com
info@pastryineurope.com

**Directors**
Norbert Koreman, Carine Van Steen,
Joost van Roosmalen

**Publisher/Chief Editor**
Norbert Koreman

**Assistant Chief Editor**
Joost van Roosmalen

**Edting Team**
Danny Janssen, Hans Kennis,
Jeroen van Oijen, Philippe Schroeven,
Etienne Van Steenberghe, Hans Heiloo

**Photography**
Norbert Koreman, Dirk Kerstens, Peter Staes

**Administrator**
Carine Van Steen

**Design**
Geert Dijkers

**Pre-press**
Anja Nelis

**Translations**
Elly Driessen, Don Genova

Pastry in Europe has been carefully edited
and accumulated. Neither the publisher nor
editors are responsible for the complete
accuracy of information, which is only meant
to give explanation. Therefore they will not
accept any liability whatsoever, derived from
the reader's interpretation and actions or
decisions, based on the given information.

The required ingredients in this book will
not always be available worldwide. The law
in certain countries might even restrict
some ingredients, materials, equipment and
techniques. Therefore we advise you to
strictly abide by the rules and regulations
in your country.

**Metric system**
The recipes given are based on the metric
system, which is used all over the European
continent.  Please refer to the conversion table
on our website: www.pastryineurope.com.

# meditations of the chief-editor

For many years we have been active on the Dutch, Belgian and French markets with our glossy culinary magazines Culinaire Saisonnier and Patisserie & Desserts. Our team of editors, all of them professional chefs and pâtissiers, travel constantly throughout Europe to look for fascinating subjects and are accompanied by the best photographers. It has been my dream for many years to publish Pastry in Europe all over the world in English and this is the result.

Compared to the United States and Canada, Europe is an interesting compilation of different cultures. You could never compare Germany with France or Denmark with Spain. It goes even further than that. Very small countries like the Netherlands and Belgium have even varied cultures in each province. If you want to travel from one city in Canada to another you probably need a plane. That is different in Europe where everything is done by car. From our head office in Schilde (Belgium) it takes us three hours to drive to Paris (France), one and a half hour to Dusseldorf (Germany), the same time to Amsterdam (Holland) and within five hours we can be in Switzerland. That makes Europe so fascinating. After every hundred kilometers traveling, you will find a different language, different people and a different culture. Pastry in Europe is a reflection of these great differences.

From now on we will publish Pastry in Europe annually with the most beautiful and interesting reportages we have done in Europe. From Belgium to Italy, from Denmark to Spain, from France to Switzerland, from anywhere in Europe you will see how pâtisserie has been a prominent part of food culture and how many recipes are centuries old. But there has also been a movement toward an ultramodern Europe where pâtisserie has gone in a totally new direction. You will be able to see this every year now in Pastry in Europe. I promise that you will thoroughly enjoy it.

If you want to be informed of the new publishing date for 2010, please check our website **www.PastryInEurope.com** Also, if you send us your e-mail address we will make sure you get this information.

*Norbert Koreman*
*Publisher*

Philippe Conticini

# Being creative

# is simple

It is rare, but some people are already plugged into their future greatness when they are born. Mozart could write a symphony when he was five years old. Einstein was a toddler when he showed interest in relativity. Michelangelo was playing with a hammer and chisel in his crib. Even in our profession of pastry we have found a star, where natural talent and intuition merged together at birth.

Conticini is a special case. Every time you feel you've figured out what he's thinking, he is way ahead of you. His father was a restaurant owner and he had only one passion and that was the candy shop. No wonder he chose to go into pâtisserie. After he finished school, he started to work for Alain Dutournier, who taught him the hot kitchen. Next, he was an apprentice-pâtissier at Maxim's and later he was hired as commis-pâtissier at Gray d'Albion. However, Philippe wanted to go even deeper and took a job at a famous pâtisserie in Paris, Peltier. After that, he and his brother decided to take over his father's restaurant, La Table d'Anvers, in Paris. It was 1986, when the adventure really started. By that time, Philippe finally felt he could take care of himself. With him in the pâtisserie and brother Christian in the hot kitchen, the business soon received a Michelin star. During that time Philippe started to see pâtisserie in a totally different way. He started playing with salt and also used more spices. This was as yet unheard of in the eighties. But salt and spices were not enough for Philippe. He felt that there were too many limitations on a dish, with always the same textures over hundreds of years. If it doesn't look good horizontally, why not do it vertically? But then you need support, so why not use glasses? Indeed, by presenting his desserts in glasses, he was able to change the textures. At that time it was considered a revolution, but soon after, the whole world copied him. In 1991, he was chosen by GaultMillau as pâtissier of the year, and his desserts were quite famous. But the adventure with his brother was over. The still-young Philippe wanted to go his own way and there was too much to consider. Life moved quickly. He became a consultant for the agro-sector, wrote books, and had his own TV show. Philippe created and created some more. He and Pierre Hermé became partners and together they started Art et Dessert, to promote pâtisserie in general.

## Frolicking in the kitchen

A bet has caused Philippe to play in the hot kitchen. He became the chef of Restaurant Petrossian in Paris, and kept his little business Philippe Consult going. At Petrossian, the world discovered that the marriage between sweet and salt was complete. Hot as well as cold dishes were presented in glasses and he gave his guests a chance to experience an adventure in tastes. He called it Rock 'n Roll. The hot kitchen, run by a pâtissier, received a star the first year. It is common that the pâtisserie has all the confitures and compôtes while the hot kitchen keeps the mustard and the mayonnaise. But Philippe, at Petrossian, maintained all components have the same function and methods. He used rasp-berries in a tart, but also in filet mignon, which he stuffed with octopus. Everything from the cold and hot kitchen were used for all kinds of dishes. In 1995, the New York Times wrote: "Conticini has removed the walls between pâtisserie and the kitchen." Philippe finally left Petrossian and devoted himself totally to consulting. Creating new concepts was the only thing he still wanted to do. Peltier became his client and Philippe,

who once worked there as a commis, revived the old house. In the meantime, he also coached the French pastry team to a world championship at Coupe du Monde!

## More than that

We are now at Exceptions Gourmandes, the business that Philippe opened in 2004. Here, for the first time in his life, he is in seventh heaven, He now has the tools in hand to knock down all the little houses of pâtisserie. He does that by creating new pastries every day and the circle of customers is large. Restaurants, shops, the industry, he has a solution for everyone. An example? The firm Ferrero asked Philippe if he could do something with their hazelnut-chocolate spread, Nutella. The result was a book that became famous in France: Sensation Nutella. He worked magic by reviving a very mundane product in dozens of spectacular creations. We thought that his book Tentations would give us a good impression of the standard that Philippe now carries. Wrong! This sold out book was published just four years ago but Conticini has again moved on. We have become genuine good friends with Philippe. He says he is grateful that we discovered him in Belgium and the Netherlands since for a Frenchman, the world stops in Paris. Our creativity appeals to him and gives him ideas.

In his atelier in Paris, a lab of hundreds of square meters, we meet chef Pascal, the big chocolate specialist, Alain, the chef-pâtissier, and André the chef. Together with the master they form the basis for Exceptions Gourmandes. We were very curious, so we asked Philippe if we could work with him for a few days, the best way to observe his philosophy. Philippe agreed and on one occasion we became part of a reception outside his shop: "Catering doesn't mean that we have to present cold and hot items on a plate, and then have servers offer these to guests. No, it should be a spectacle, something that surprises the guests." And that didn't say much. Conticini has even developed a stand for the siphon, so that anything can be made immediately. Lollipops made of lamb and chicken, cotton candy, a line with a straw of Nutella powder. Sweet, salt, bitter, sour, the maestro creates magic with components as if it is nothing. The guests at the reception get more than thirty intriguing items; it is a true cornucopia. Behind the scenes, Alain is finishing his straight pâtisserie. Straight, because you can put a ruler next to it and won't find one millimeter difference. And we all shout together: "That is real pâtisserie!"

## Philosophy

We asked what the difference is for Conticini between yesterday and today. Philippe: "Creativity has always been my passion. Just yesterday you saw the croissant and the chou à la crème. In the early days, these were created by people who were thinking outside the box. At first they were regarded with skepticism, but today they are classics. Today sweet is becoming unlimited. We live in a hyper-communication era. People want to consume, want excellent service, want to be surprised and want constant renewal. People want everything at the same instant. The world has become a small village, it's the reason why we have an open mind. Everyone has gotten the right to express himself freely. If we don't forget to respect the profession and the traditions, we can use the world today as a fresh start. We then go back to our own feelings and emotions. Creativity helps to express ourselves." But some take that more seriously than others? "Because we are all different, our creations are familiar to us, but might be peculiar to somebody else. That makes this time so

fascinating." What about pâtisserie in the near future? According to Conticini, our creations will get simpler, but with more meaning to the design. We will always have to come up with new ideas to keep the public interested. We have to expand our mind. But let us not forget that pâtisserie should not be elite. Pleasures should be accessible to everyone. "Whenever I dipped my finger in the cream and chocolate, as a child, I realized that pâtisserie is deeply connected to pleasure. Just like everyone else, I have had some past. There was a time that I was looking for complexity, but simplicity came back. However… I see flavours as colours. To get a deeper red, a painter needs more colour, while the end result is still red. If I want to give a strawberry a stronger taste, I look for additives, but the strawberry will still taste like a strawberry, nothing else." Philippe often uses the word creativity. Does that not come naturally to everyone? "It is very simple. But to discover that creativity is simple, that takes years."

**www.conticini.com**

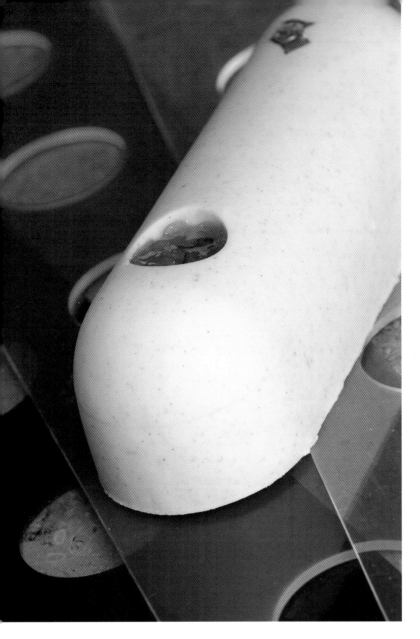

## Buche B

*White chocolate mousse:* 580 g white chocolate, 230 g crème fleurette (cooking cream with only 20% fat content, which will not separate at hot temperature), 26 g gelatin, 160 g paté a bombe, 280 g Italian meringue, 980 whipped cream.
*Dried apricot jam:* 130 g dried apricots, 10 g butter, 5 g sugar, 120 g lemon juice, 250 g apricot jam, 5 g basil, 2 g pectin, 2 g sugar.
*Nut biscuit:* 60 g icing sugar, 30 g walnut powder, 30 g almond powder, 100 g eggs, 30 g flour, 100 g egg whites, 20 g sugar, 35 g butter.
*Coconut praliné:* 120 g white chocolate, 120 g cocoa butter, 280 g almond and hazelnut praliné, 60 g shredded coconut, 110 g feuillantine (small crunchy chocolate slivers).

*For the biscuit:* Beat eggs and icing sugar until they turn white. Beat egg whites and sugar until stiff. Clarify the butter. Mix the three mixtures together. Spread dough on non-greased paper and bake in a convection oven for 7 minutes at 200ºC/390ºF.
*For the jam:* Cut the dried apricots in small cubes. Mix the sugar and butter and sauté apricots in this. Deglaze with the lemon juice and add the jam. Let boil for a few minutes and add the pectin mixed with the 2 g sugar. Cool and add the finely chopped basil.
*For the praliné:* Melt the cocoa butter with the white chocolate. Mix the shredded coconut with the feuillantine. Add both mixtures to the praliné, roll up to 2mm in a baking frame and put in the fridge. Take a buche-form (log shaped form) for four people. Temper the white chocolate and coat the inside of the form with it. Let crystallize, cut off the excess off the chocolate and keep at room temperature. Slice two nut biscuits and one coconut praliné in the form of the buche. For the white chocolate mousse: Make a ganache with the white chocolate and the cream. Add the pre-soaked gelatin. Cool and add the bombe dough and the meringue. Then carefully add the whipped cream. Use a piping bag to cover the bottom of the buche form with chocolate mousse and then a biscuit. Add another layer of mousse, and let it set in the fridge. Then cover it with jam and a praliné. Top again with mousse and finish with the second biscuit. Put in the fridge and when set, invert on a plate.

### Banana croquettes

*Banana mixture:* 450 g peeled bananas, 25 g lemon juice,
1 g cinnamon, 1 g ginger, 12 g sugar, 50 g flour.
*Bread crumbs:* 200 g almond powder, 200 g eggs,
250 g breadcrumbs.
*Garnish:* Nutella.

Mash the bananas with a fork. Add the sugar, spices, lemon juice, and the sifted flour and mix to a smooth dough. In a flexipan mould dough into half balls. Put the balls together and put in the freezer for one hour. Then, dip the balls in the beaten eggs, then in the almond powder and then in the breadcrumbs, repeat once more. Keep in the freezer until ready to deep fry for 2 minutes at 170°C/340°F.

## Caramel Indian

*Ingredients:* 988 g Indian caramel mousse, 300 g mango chutney, 132 g soft caramel ganache, 152 g coconut biscuit, 40 g five-spices syrup, 140 g praliné feuilleté curry (crushed wafers), 40 g milky velvet (white chocolate that is melted with cocoa butter), gold leaf.

**Indian caramel mousse:** 470 g caramel bombe dough, 60 g caramel Italian foam, 425 g crème fleurette, 2 g salt, 8 g Patrelle aroma (100% glucose based golden clear colouring, with the advantage of being able to colour instantly, without blackening or leaving a deposit), 10 g vanilla extract, 3 g red colouring.

**Caramel bombe dough:** 265 caramel sauce, 200 g running egg yolks, 20 g gelatin sheets.

**Caramel sauce:** 70 g water, 141 g icing sugar, 55 g water to deglaze.

**Caramel foam:** 100 g caramel syrup, 70 g egg white, and 30 g water.

**Caramel syrup:** 25 g water, 55 g icing sugar, 20 g water to deglaze.

**Mango chutney:** 200 g lemon balm syrup, 20 g lemon juice, 150 g mango flesh, cut in cubes, 10 g sugar, 4 g pectin.

**Lemon balm syrup:** 130 g fresh orange juice, 35 g lemon juice, 5 g sprigs of lemon balm, 5 g white vinegar, 20 g sugar, 1 g five-spice, 1 dash of star anise powder, 3 g star anise.

**Soft caramel ganache:** 32 g sugar, 27 g glucose, 35 g water, 4 g butter, 60 g crème fleurette, 35 g white chocolate, 0,3 g salt, 0,2 g vanilla extract.

**Coconut biscuit:** 105 g fresh eggs, 40 g running egg yolks, 50 g sugar, 1 g vanilla powder, 20 g coconut powder, 40 g flour T 55, 40 g corn starch, 25 g shredded coconut, 15 g lukewarm clarified butter.

**Five-spices syrup:** 80 g syrup à 30o, 2 g five-spice, 10 g lemon juice, 40 g water.

**Praliné feuilleté carry:** 14 g guava couverture, 20 g cocoa butter, 90 g praliné 60/40, 20 g feuillantine, 1 g curry, 0,1 g ginger powder, 1 g hazelnut oil.

**Milky velvet:** 100 g milk chocolate, 70 g cocoa butter.

*Coconut biscuit:* Whip up the eggs, the egg yolks and the sugar. Mix sifted flour, cornstarch, coconut powder and vanilla powder. Stir both mixtures together. Add the shredded coconut and the clarified butter, spread out on a baking sheet to 5 mm thickness and bake in a convection oven at 180oC/350oF for 7 minutes. For the lemon balm syrup, bring all ingredients to a boil, and pour through a sieve and set aside.

*For the mango chutney:* boil the lemon balm syrup, add the mango cubes and the lemon juice and cook slowly for 30 minutes. Mix the sugar with the pectin and let thicken with the chutney.

*For the caramel syrup and the caramel sauce:* Caramelize both separately with water and sugar and deglaze with water. Put both aside.

*For the caramel foam:* boil the caramel syrup with the water to 121°C /250°F. Beat the egg whites very stiff; add the warm syrup slowly. Keep beating until it is cooled off and set aside. For the caramel bombe dough: Heat the caramel sauce, whip the egg yolks and add to the warm sauce. Keep beating it and add the pre-soaked gelatin. Keep going until the mixture has reached 35oC/95oF.

*For the praliné feuilleté:* melt the chocolate and the cocoa butter, add the oil and the spices, pour all of it on the praliné. Keep stirring and add the feuillantine. Pour the mixture between two rulers to 4 mm thickness. Put in the fridge and cut it afterwards in a preferred form.

*For the five-spice syrup:* Bring all ingredients to a boil and let cool. Cut the coconut biscuit the size of the chosen form and moisten with the five-spice syrup.

*For the caramel mousse:* Lightly whip the cream and mix with the caramel bombe dough together with the salt, the aromas and colouring. Add this mousse to the caramel foam and set aside in the fridge.

*For the soft caramel ganache:* caramelize the sugar, glucose and water, deglaze with the cream and add the butter. Pour this mixture on the white chocolate with the salt and the vanilla extract. Fill the form with 1 cm of the caramel mousse. Put in the freezer for a few minutes to firm up the mousse. With a piping bag, pipe the mango chutney on the caramel mousse and cover with caramel ganache. Then put on another layer of caramel mousse, followed by a coconut biscuit. Again add another layer of mousse, followed with praliné feuilleté. Top with the rest of the mousse and finish with a coconut biscuit. Put in the fridge so it can all set.

*For the milky velvet:* Heat the white chocolate with the cocoa butter and pour in a baking gun. Take the tart out of the form and spray the whole tart with the gun to get a velvety effect. Garnish with pieces of coloured chocolate and gold leaves.

## Café d' écume

For 25 pieces:

*Coffee foam:* 125 g espresso, 40 g coffee beans, 75 g unsweetened condensed milk, 200 g whole milk, 50 g crème fleurette, 20 g egg yolk, 20 g sugar, 1 dash of licorice powder, 1 g trablit (liquid coffee extract), 1 g fleur de sel.
*Chocolate caramel:* 100 g sugar, 80 g cream, 10 g butter, 180 g pure chocolate, 50 g water, 700 g 2% milk, 70 g cream.
*Condiment:* 20 g almond oil, cocoa powder.

*For the foam:* heat the milk and the condensed milk, add the coffee beans, let stand for 4 minutes and pour through a fine mesh sieve. Add the espresso and the cream and heat to 80°C/175°F. Beat egg yolks and sugar and pour the hot espresso over it. Add the spices and trablit; pour in a siphon and let cool. Add a charger to the siphon and let rest in the fridge for one hour before using. *For the chocolate caramel:* melt the sugar without water, deglaze with cream and add butter. Then add the water and the pure chocolate, let melt slowly and add the milk. Stir while you bring it to a boil and lastly add the cream. Fill half of it in a little glass flute, carefully add 2 mm almond oil and finish with the coffee foam. Sprinkle with cocoa powder and serve immediately with a small straw.

## Entre Deux

*Hazelnut-chocolate biscuit:* 95 g egg yolks, 45 g eggs, 80 g almond paste, 25 g trimoline, 45 g flour, 35 g hazelnut powder, 30 g butter, 95 g egg white.
*Ganache of pure chocolate:* 230 g crème fleurette, 200 g pure chocolate 70%, 40 g butter, 10 g syrup 30o, 1 vanilla bean.
*Insert of sour strawberry:* 350 g strawberries, 100 g sugar, 50 g lemon juice, 1 g salt, 15 g pectin, 15 g sugar.
*Crusty chocolate:* 30 g pure chocolate, 10 g cocoa butter, 280 g praliné almond hazelnut, 80 g feuillantine.
*Black velvet:* 100 g pure chocolate, 50 g cocoa butter.

*For the biscuit:* Beat the eggs with the almond paste, the egg yolks and the trimoline with an electric beater. Put the flour, the cocoa powder and the hazelnut powder through a sieve. Melt the butter. Beat the egg whites until quite stiff. Blend the almond paste with the flour mixture, add the butter and than (carefully) add the egg whites. Pour on a baking sheet to 5mm thick and bake in a convection oven for 10 minutes at 170°C/340°F.
*For the crust:* Melt the chocolate and the cocoa butter and add all the ingredients. Roll the mixture to a thickness of 3mm between two sheets of wax paper and cool in the fridge. For the insert: Mix strawberries with the lemon juice, the sugar, and the salt and cook slowly until the strawberries are soft and done. Mix 15 g sugar with the pectin, add to the strawberries, let thicken and reserve. For the ganache: Heat the cream and pour over the chopped chocolate. Mix together carefully and add the butter, the vanilla bean and the syrup. Let cool to room temperature. Cut the biscuit in four even triangles and the crust in two same-sized triangles. For the base, cut two rectangles of the biscuit, crunch one and make one crust almost the same length as the triangles. Build the elements up with the fillings, just like a sandwich and let rest in the fridge for a while. Release the velvet with the baking gun. Place a gold leaf on one of the triangles.

For the sweet dough: Make a dough with the ingredients as mentioned, let rest for one hour in the fridge, and roll out in a tart forms of 85 mm in diameter. Bake at the bottom of the oven at 180ºC/350ºF until they look golden. Wash the rice and cook this carefully in the milk with the sugar and vanilla. Cool, and slowly add the whipped cream; set aside in the fridge.

For the jelly: Heat the water with the honey and the sugar. Dissolve the chestnut purée in 6 g water. Add the purée, the Armagnac, the vanilla and the pre-soaked gelatin to the syrup; push through a sieve and then through a coffee filter.

For the chestnut compôte: Mix the cream with the chestnut purée, add the armagnac and the vanilla and store in the fridge.

For the amarena jam: Cook all the ingredients together; mix the pectin with 1g of sugar and add. Let thicken and line 5 g jam in half moon flexi pan shapes. Put in the freezer. With a piping bag put a layer of 1 cm on the bottom of the tart, put the cherry insert in the center and put 15 minutes in the fridge. Fill the rest of the tart form with the rice porridge, smooth the top and let rest for 1 hour in the fridge. Put a rhodoïd leaf (or baking paper) around the tart; there should be an edge of 5 mm above the tart. Pour the still liquidy but cold jelly on top and put again in the fridge for 15 minutes. Finish with a chestnut dipped in caramel, a chocolate decoration and gold leaves.

## Chestnut tart

For 10 pieces: 300 g sweet dough, 50 g insert amarena (sour black cherry) jam, 300 g chestnut compôte, 250 g rice porridge, 150 g chestnut jelly.

For the sweet dough: 80 g butter, 35 g icing sugar, 35 g almond powder, 25 g eggs, 130 g flour T55.

For the insert amarena jam: 15 g cherries griotte amarena, 7 g water, 0.5 g cinnamon powder. 6 g cherry jam, 0,5 g candied orange peel, 15 g griotte pitless cherries, 4 g red wine, 1 g pectin, and 1 g sugar.

For the chestnut compôte: 22 g armagnac, 7 g liquid vanilla, 135 g chestnut purée, 135 g chestnut paste.

For the rice porridge: 185 g 2% milk, 30 g Arborio rice, 15 g sugar, 1.5 g vanilla bean, 10 g whipped cream.

For the chestnut jelly: 95 g water, 16 g chestnut honey, 11 g sugar, 6 g water, 17 g chestnut purée, 1.5 g armagnac, 0.5 g vanilla, 1.5 g gelatin.

*Even snuffing is possible with Philippe. With the Paco-Jet or Frix-Air (turbo mixers) you can make a bit of powder in no time.*

*Enoteca Pinchiorri*

# Loretta Fanella

The city of Florence has a restaurant many people consider to be the best in Italy. Enoteca Pinchiorri was started by Giorgio Pinchiorri and his wife Annie Féolde. She used to run the kitchen and was one of the first women who was awarded three Michelin stars in Italy. They still have three Michelin stars although she decided to remove herself a bit more from the kitchen, where chefs Italo Rossie and Riccardo Monco now run the show. The pâtisserie is managed by a young woman, just 26 years old, named Loretta. Loretta is like a little pearl and has been the chef-pâtissier of the restaurant for over a year. She seems shy, but judging by her resumé, she knows what she wants. She started at a simple restaurant in Verona and went from there to Cracco-Peck in Milan, where she worked for two years. Then she moved to El Bulli where she worked for three years with the brothers Adrià. After that it was time to return to her native country and she arrived in Florence full of experience and knowledge. She supervises four staff in her pâtisserie corner that occupies half of the restaurant kitchen. She also has her own baker and chocolatier.

## Impact

Her desserts are a feast for the eyes and certainly also stand out for the taste. She describes her style as natural and that shows in different ways. A garden with flowers, a basket full of herbs or the inspiration of the sea. You won't find complicated El Bulli desserts as she has her own style. Loretta: " I learned a lot at El Bulli. I don't have the style they use, but I do believe in their philosophy. At my previous job it was a matter of new flavours and techniques, but I prefer classic flavours in combination with new techniques." The chef knows the place of a dessert on a menu: "After a menu with many courses you should not serve a heavy dessert. My desserts are light and have a great taste. It is the creation that counts. A dessert is the last impression the guests see."

**www.enotecapinchiorri.com**

## The Garden

*For the crumble of green tea:* 100 g butter, 100 g flour,
100 g cane sugar, 4 g green tea powder.
*For the mint jelly:* 40 g mint leaves, 15 g water, 15 g sugar,
2 g agar-agar.
*For the orange jelly:* 100 g orange juice, 15 g sugar, 15 g water,
zest of 1 orange, 3 g gelatin.
*For the mint and basil ice cream:* 250 g water, 200 g cream,
100 g glucose, 3 g stabilizer, 65 g sugar, 150 g mint leaves,
80 g basil leaves.

For the crumble mix all ingredients till smooth and put in the freezer.
Using a stainless steel rasp grate a bit of the dough on a baking sheet
lined with parchment paper and bake for 4 minutes at 120ºC/250ºF.
Roll the cake to create fine crumbs. For the mint jelly blanch the mint
leaves and mix them with the water and sugar. Pour the mix through a
sieve and dissolve the agar-agar in it. Pour on a flat sheet and cut into
small circles. For the orange jelly heat the orange juice, sugar, water and
zest. Dissolve gelatin in it and drain. For the ice cream, blanch mint and
basil and cool in ice water.  Mix the leaves with the rest of the ingredients
and heat to 80ºC/175ºF. Pour the mixture in frix beakers and frix (spin)
before use. Roll a quenelle of ice cream through the crumble. Sprinkle
also some crumble on the plate and garnish with flowers.

## The flower puzzle

*For the lavender mousse:* 250 g milk, 10 g lavender, 50 g sugar,
2 gelatin leaves, 130 g cream
*For the mousse of the strawberry flowers:* 250 g cream,
25 g infusion of strawberry flowers, 50 g sugar, 2 gelatin leaves,
130 g cream.
*For the pannacotta of karkade (hibiscus flowers):* 300 g milk,
18 g karkade infusion, 75 g sugar, 3 g gelatin powder.
*For the chamomile jelly:* 300 g water, 15 g chamomile,
50 g sugar, 2 gelatin leaves.
*For the rose cake:* 300 g butter, 200 g sugar, 2 egg yolks,
500 g flour, 1 g salt, 20 g rose powder.
*For the verbena tea:* 250 g water, 15 g sugar, 5 g dried verbena.

Lavender mousse: Infuse the lavender with the milk and sugar, pass
through a sieve and add pre-soaked gelatin. Whip the cream lightly and
mix with the lavender mixture. Fill the puzzle forms with the mixture,
freeze and then loosen. Prepare the strawberry mousse the same way.
For the pannacotta cook the milk and sugar with the karkade infusion.
Cool slightly and dissolve gelatin in it, pour in puzzle moulds (available
in specialized cookshops)  and set aside. Brew chamomile and sugar
with water for 4 minutes, pour through a sieve and dissolve gelatin in it.
Pour mixture in puzzle moulds.
Mix ingredients for the rose cake, pour mixture in puzzle forms and bake
in the oven at 175ºC/350ºF. Cool and remove from the forms. For the
verbena tea, boil water and sugar, add the verbena, brew and cool. Put the
puzzle pieces together and serve with the verbena tea.

## Autumn

*For the honey cream filling:* 500 g cream, 50 g honey.
*For the figs:* 4 red figs, the honey cream filling.
*For the caramel jelly:* 100 g sugar, 150 g water, 5 g vegetal gelatin (Sosa).
*For the cinnamon cake:* 300 g butter, 140 g sugar, 1 egg yolk, 50 g cornstarch, 500 g flour, 5 g cinnamon powder.
*For the chocolate sauce:* 100 g sugar, 10 g glucose, 30 g water, 20 g cocoa mass.
*For the fig ice cream:* 200 g fresh peeled figs, 50 g sugar water.

For the filling reduce cream to one-third and add the honey. Peel the figs, scoop out the centre and fill each fig with 20 g honey cream filling and freeze. Caramel jelly: Mix water and sugar and boil to caramelize and add the gelatin. Dip the frozen figs twice in it.

Cinnamon cake: Mix the butter and sugar for 10 minutes with the flat beater and beat together with the egg yolk. Mix the flour, cornstarch and cinnamon through the mixture. Let this rest in the fridge. Spread on a baking sheet and bake the cake in the oven at 165°C/330°F. Crumble cake when cool. For the chocolate sauce cook all ingredients at 117°C/242°F except the cocoa mass. Take off of the burner, add the cocoa mass and stir well. For the ice cream puree the figs with the sugar water. Divide into frix beakers, freeze and frix (spin) before use.

## Spiral of lemon marshmallow with blackberries and lemon sorbet

*For the lemon marshmallow:* 40 g egg whites, 100 g fresh lemon juice, 4 gelatin leaves, 180 g sugar, 80 g water.
*For the blackberry puree:* 100 g blackberries, 20 g sugar.
*For the lemon sorbet:* 150 g water, 150 g sugar, 80 g glucose, 50 g invert sugar, 250 g lemon juice, 300 g water.
*For blackberry segments:* fresh blackberries.

For the lemon marshmallow mix boil water and sugar at 115°C/240°F and cool to 80°C/175°F.  Beat egg whites and pour a thin stream of syrup into this mixture. Dissolve gelatin in the lemon juice and add to the egg whites.  For the puree, mix blackberries with sugar until smooth and set aside in the fridge. For the sorbet, dissolve sugar in water, glucose and invert sugar, heat to 80°C/175°F and add lemon juice and water. Pour into frix beakers and spin before use. For the segments freeze the berries and separate them in half between two sheets of paper using a rolling pin.  Pipe a spiral of the marshmallow mixture on a plate and fill the spiral with the blackberry puree. Roll a ball of sorbet through the berry segments and garnish with flowers.

# Noma
### The new Scandinavian gastronomy

**During a visit to Copenhagen it was difficult for us to avoid visiting Noma. Chef René Redzepi, who is considered among the top 10 chefs in the world, demonstrated in a young and most innovative way his respect for the region and let us taste the exclusive flavors of the local food in Scandinavia. During a full course menu, herbs, flowers and plants you have never seen or have never dared to eat passed in front of our eyes. He is not afraid of modern techniques, they are even invented here, but above all clean and authentic tastes are top priority.**

Today we are here to visit a Canadian chef-pâtissier and that is why we are visiting the Danish capital. Daniel Burns grew up on the East Coast of Canada near Halifax where he took his education, but then moved to Vancouver, a city with a lot more culinary pizzazz. He worked another year with famous Canadian chef Susur Lee in Toronto until his British girlfriend took him back to her country. Not a bad choice since it gave him an opportunity to work at St. JOHN restaurant and The Fat Duck. But when a friend moved to Copenhagen to work at Noma, Daniel

decided to follow him. He has been working there for over two years as chef-pâtissier in the very busy kitchen. Because Daniel is one of those job hoppers, we asked him why he is still at this same address? "This business is constantly developing and though many chefs claim they cook according to the season, here it really happens. René feels strongly about that and would not want it any different. We have a good position in the market and therefore have access to the best and freshest produce available. The cooking style is light and clean. The chef's food is very inspirational and that's why I want to stay here for a while."
Our chef-pâtissier uses the same style in his desserts. "I hardly use any chocolate or dairy and the sweet content is as low as possible. As pâtissier you should adapt your desserts to the food the guest has eaten. Therefore I use savoury ingredients and many frozen items. I like playing with textures and temperatures. When I decorate a plate I do this very consciously and think of the way the guest will eat it. The order in which it is eaten determines how the flavours will fit as they are meant to be. You almost have to guide the guest through the dishes to get the optimum effect."

**www.noma.dk**

## Sheep yogurt and sorrel

*For 4 people:* green anise seeds, olive oil.
*For the mousse of sheep yogurt:* 300 g sheep yogurt, 3 gelatin leaves, 250 g whipped cream, 150 g egg white, 50 g sugar.
*For the granita of sorrel:* 2kg water, 600 g sugar, 26 bunches of sorrel, 220 g lemon juice.
*For the nougat tuile:* 450 g glucose, 575 g fondant powder.

For the mousse warm a bit of the yogurt and dissolve the pre-soaked gelatin in it. Mix well with the rest of the yogurt and beat egg whites with the sugar.
Combine yogurt, whipped cream and meringue and put in a piping bag.

For the granita boil water and sugar until it is dissolved and let cool. Pick the leaves of the sorrel, wash thoroughly and dry completely. Whisk the dried leaves and the sugar syrup in a blender until smooth and pass through a sieve; add the lemon juice and place in a container in a blastchiller. Scrape it loose regularly and then put aside in a normal freezer. For the tuile cook glucose and fondant powder to 130ºC/265ºF, pour on a silpat and cool. Grind to a fine powder in a food processor and sprinkle a thin layer on a dry silpat. Cut in desired shapes and sprinkle lightly with green anise seed. Bake 3 minutes in a regular oven at 160ºC/320ºF. Draw a line on a plate with the mousse, put on a straight rectangular tuile and scoop a generous amount of granita on the side. Finish with a few drops of olive oil.

## Walnuts and dried red fruit

*For 4 people:* powder of dried red fruit, roasted oatmeal crumbs, sweetened whipped cream.

*For the walnut ice cream:* 1900 g walnuts (blanched 4x) 3500 g milk, 900 g cream, 800 g trimoline, 350 g sugar, 12 g salt, 14 g ice Stabilizer.

*For the walnut powder mix:* 300 g walnut praliné, 35 g walnut oil, 200 g maltose, icing sugar, salt.

For the ice cream heat the milk, cream and walnuts and simmer for 10 minutes. Add the rest of the ingredients and beat in the blender until smooth. Cool and beat to get coarse ice cream using liquid nitrogen. For the walnut mix beat the oil and maltose with a hand mixer to get a light lumpy mixture Add the praliné and bring to taste with salt and icing sugar. Deep-fry the lumps in liquid nitrogen and grind to powder in a thermo blender. Create quenelles of whipped cream and sprinkle with the different powders and crumbs and serve immediately.

## Rhubarb and Beets

*For 4 people:* granita of yogurt, yogurt powder
*For the beet sorbet:* 750 g strained beet juice, 450 g sugar syrup,
30 g lemon juice, 7 g gelatin leaves
*For the beet jelly:* 500 g strained beet juice, 6 g agar-agar,
4 g gelatin leaves
*For the rhubarb compôte:* 750 g washed and peeled rhubarb,
450 g icing sugar.
*For the rhubarb mousse:* 400 g strained rhubarb juice,
80 g yogurt, 6 gelatin leaves, 225 g whipped cream, 100 g egg
white, 45 g crystal sugar.
*For the yogurt tuile:* 900 g glucose, 1150 g fondant powder.

For the sorbet heat a little bit of syrup and dissolve the pre-soaked
gelatin in it. Take off the burner and add the rest of the ingredients.
Pour in frix or paco beakers and freeze. Afterwards spin to get a
smooth sorbet. For the jelly heat the pre-soaked gelatin with the juice
to 80°C/175°F, add the agar-agar and bring to a boil. Boil for 20 seconds
and pour a very thin layer on a plate.

For the compôte cut the rhubarb in very fine brunoise, mix with the icing
sugar and vacuum (sous vide). Cook for 28 minutes at 80°C/175°F in the
oven with steam and cool in ice water. Pour the mixture in pot, bring to a
boil and cook for 2 minutes. Take off the burner and cover firmly with
saran wrap. Let stand for 5 minutes and pour through a chinois. Press
down with a wooden spoon to get the right texture.

For the mousse heat a bit of the yogurt and mix with the pre-soaked
gelatin. Add the rest of the yogurt and mix with the rhubarb juice.
Beat egg whites with sugar and mix with the yogurt and whipped cream.
Put in piping bags. For the tuile cook glucose and fondant powder to
130°C/265°F and pour on a silpat. Cool and grind to a smooth powder.
Pour a very thin layer on a silpat and bake for 3 minutes in a regular
oven at 160°C/320°F. Break in pieces and dip in the yogurt powder.
Put compote and sorbet in a deep soup plate, cover with a piece of jelly
and finish with the crunchy yogurt and granita.

La Table du Lancaster

# Keiko

# Nagae

What would you do if you were studying law at the Sorbonne but your passion is really pâtisserie? Keiko made this her life history. This chef pâtissier is a young lady from Tokyo. She originally came to Paris to study and earned some extra money in the evening in the "cold" kitchen. Once she finished her studies, she decided to make her passion her profession. To further educate herself she went to the famous hotel school in Lausanne, then the Cordon Bleu Cooking School. After apprenticing at the very well known Pâtissier Ladurée in Paris, she began working for Pierre Gagnaire at Sketches in London. Back in Paris she started in the kitchen of Yannick Alleno in Hotel Meurice. There she met Michel Troisgros, who was busy working on a new Lancaster project. As a result she became his chef-pâtissier. In the beginning the dessert menu and creations were dictated by Michel Troisgros, but that is now past. Michel trusts Keiko blindly. What is the most important component in her desserts? Keiko: "All my creations evolve around fruit, with full respect for the seasons."

www.hotel-lancaster.fr

## Around the Orange

*For the orange shortbread:* 280 g butter, 100 g icing sugar, 60 g boiled egg yolk passed through a sieve, 1 g fleur de sel, 50 g almond powder, 300 g flour, 3 orange peels.
*For the orange in caramel:* 150 g sugar, 200 g orange juice, 5 oranges.
*For the orange crème:* 200 g egg yolk, 170 g sugar, 25 g orange zest, 135 g orange juice, 30 g lemon juice, 2 g gelatin, 200 g butter.
*For the orange sorbet ice cream:* 750 g orange juice, 50 g sugar, 3 g stabilizer, 60 g glucose powder, 8 ml water.

For the shortbread, make a dough with the ingredients and let rest. Roll out, cut with a ring and bake in the oven until golden brown. For the caramel, cut segments out of the oranges. Caramelize the sugar dry and deglaze with warm orange juice. Pour this over the segments and cool in the fridge. Prepare the crème as a crème anglaise and cook au bain-marie. For the sorbet ice cream, heat syrup with sugar, water, the glucose and the stabilizer. Cool and mix with the orange juice. Let rest for a few hours and spin the ice cream. Drain the orange segments. Place a piece of shortbread on a plate and put a ring on top. Put some segments in the ring in the form of a rosette and finish with orange crème. Take the ring off and cover with a quenelle of sorbet ice cream. Garnish with some caramel sauce and a dried orange slice.

## Mangococo

*For the mango coulis:* 200 g mango purée, 10 g limejuice.
*For the tapioca cocos:* 200 g coconut milk, 250 g coconut purée,
25 g sugar, 50 g Japanese pearls.
*For the coconut florentines:* 125 g egg whites, 150 g sugar,
125 g shredded coconut, 100 g butter.
*For the light coconut foam:* 500 g coconut purée, 2 sheets of
gelatin, 2 charges.
*For the coconut sorbet ice cream:* 1 kg coconut flesh, 625 g water,
250 g sugar, 50 g trimoline, 90 g coconut extract.

For the coulis, mix both ingredients and keep in the fridge. For the
tapioca, soak the Japanese pearls in cold water, drain and cook in the
coconut milk with sugar, stirring constantly. Let cool and add the
coconut purée. For the florentines, mix butter and sugar, add the
shredded coconut and add the egg whites a little at a time. Let rest,
pour on a silpat and bake in the oven at 160ºC/320ºF. Take a glass and cut
the florentines to its size. For the foam, soak the gelatin and add the
lukewarm coconut purée. Pour in a siphon and use two chargers. For the
sorbet ice cream, make a syrup with the sugar, water and trimoline, add
the coconut flesh and coconut extract, pass through a sieve and finish in
ice cream machine. Pour some mango coulis in the bottom of a glass, put
a florentine on top and garnish with tapioca cocos. Cover with another
florentine. Garnish the edge of the glass with slices of mango and fill
the centre with pieces of mango. Add coconut foam, grate some lime peel
on it and finish with a quenelle of sorbet ice cream. Garnish with a piece
of white coconut.

## Tonka parfait with chocolate-tonka ganache

*For the tonka parfait:* 50 ml cream, 3 tonka beans, 120 g sugar, 40 g water, 150 g egg yolk.

*For the Viennese shortbread:* 420 g butter, 160 g crystal sugar, 4x dash of salt, red colouring, 80 g cocoa bean peel, 5 g vanilla powder, 100 g egg whites, 440 g flour, 20 g cocoa powder.

*For the chocolate-tonka ganache:* 250 g milk, 250 g cream, 3 tonka beans, 120 g egg yolk, 90 g coarse sugar, 300 g Guanaja chocolate.

*For the cocoa sauce:* 145 g syrup 30o, 90 g water, 45 g cocoa powder.

*For the Guanaja pieces:* Guanaja chocolate.

For the parfait, soak the tonka beans in the cream overnight. Make a syrup with the sugar and water and pour over the egg yolks. Whisk these au bain marie to a foam, take off the burner and continue whisking cold. Whip the cream and carefully add to the mixture. Pour this mixture in a rectangular baking frame. For the shortbread, prepare the dough with the listed ingredients and let rest. Roll the dough to 2 mm and cut in rectangles of 4 x 13 cm. Bake in the oven at 160°C/320°F. For the ganache, heat the milk with the cream and the tonka beans and let stand for a few minutes. Strain through a sieve and bring back to a boil. Beat the egg yolks with the sugar until white and pour the warm milk mixture over top. Cook as an anglaise to 82°C/180°F. Pour over the chocolate and whip as a ganache. For the sauce, dissolve the chocolate in the water and mix with the syrup. Temper the chocolate and pour thinly in a frame of 12 x 3 cm and another one of 12 x 1.5 cm. Place a small piece of shortbread on a plate. Cut the parfait a little smaller than the shortbread.

Pipe the ganache, using a piping bag with a serrated tip, on the slice of chocolate. Garnish with gold leaf and add the other-sized piece of chocolate. Use a small brush to apply the sauce on the plate.

# Avant Garde

Under the influence of Spanish chef Ferran Adrià and his colleague Heston Blumenthal, a new movement has started: the high tech kitchen. Hereby all culinary traditions have been faced with a challenge. Gone is the classic kitchen of Escoffier and gone is the nouvelle cuisine of Paul Bocuse. According to these avant garde artistes, it is time for new material and new techniques.

Is the Avant Garde right? Well, we expect that most of these techniques will end up in a museum in a few years! But somehow some part of this new craft will stay. Compare it to the paintings of Van Gogh, Picasso, and Dali. Although they are now in the past, the art of painting has changed because of them.

Our editor Jeroen van Oyen studied these techniques and experimented in our test kitchen. Here are the results…

*New techniques with liquid nitrogen*

# Cryo

Six years ago, when we filmed at El Bulli's restaurant, we were introduced to Cryo cooking for the very first time. After Ferran Adriá copied this technique from London's Michelin three-star chef Heston Blumenthal, the trend really took off. Another Spanish chef, El Calima's Dani Garcia, has written an entire book on the topic and in the meantime several European chefs have utilized this spectacular technique. But what do we really know about it? What aspects of the science do you have to pay attention to in your kitchen?

The air we breathe consists of 78% nitrogen. It is the most common element on earth. Nitrogen can be solid (ice), gas or liquid. Gas becomes liquid when the pressure on it is increased, or by cooling it to a very low temperature. Liquid nitrogen has been used for many years in the food and health industry, and even by bull and horse breeders to store frozen semen and embryos. Working with liquid nitrogen in gastronomy creates fantastic possibilities and is not limited to submerging a mousse to create a crunchy meringue layer. But don't treat the idea lightly; there is danger involved in using a liquid that exists at -196°C/-320°F. Don't be overconfident and expect that it is the same as deep-frying. Strictly respect the instructions you receive from your supplier. Some countries might even prohibit working with liquid nitrogen in the kitchen. Consult the laws and safety regulations in your country.

## Safety

Just as we should wear safety shoes while working in the kitchen, we should also take great precautions when working with liquid nitrogen. It is so cold that metals exposed to it can become brittle and even shatter. Always use a so-called Dewar-vat, a double-insulated stainless steel bowl.
Liquid nitrogen is much more dangerous than deep frying oil. The liquid can spatter and if you drop too much food in it, it can easily boil over. Always wear safety gloves and safety glasses, no matter how ridiculous

D09

you look. Liquid nitrogen evaporates very quickly and one liter of liquid substance can turn into 690 liters of gas. This means that you should always work in a well-ventilated area. You could faint or fall into a coma if there is too much nitrogen in the air. Again: always work in a ventilated room and remember that liquid gas is heavier than air and will be low to the ground. It's better to open a door instead of a window.

Still interested? Just take these safety precautions seriously and you can try some very interesting new possibilities: Preparation of the so-called Nitro-candies or Nitro-meringues, creating ice-cream powder with a mechanical syringe, creating thin layers of jelly by first freezing the soft products in liquid nitrogen, creating pearls of ice or Solero shots made from fruit coulis and table preparations made from sorbet.

### Nitro-cocktail Pina Colada

*Ingredients:* 200 g pineapple coulis, 100 g coconut milk, 50 g sugar water, 100 g coconut liqueur, 200 g unsweetened whipping cream.

Mix all ingredients together and add some extra liqueur or sugar water to give it more taste. Pour into a siphon and add air with a $N_2O$ charger. Put a dot of foam on a spoon and submerge it for about 15 seconds in the liquid nitrogen. Take it out with a fine scoop and serve immediately on a very cold platter.

### Ice-cream powder with white chocolate

*Ingredients:* 400 g white chocolate, 100 g cocoa butter.

Melt the white chocolate and the cocoa butter and pour into a clean electric spray painter (the same method is applied to give desserts a shiny surface with chocolate).

Spray the chocolate mixture in the liquid nitrogen and leave for several seconds. Spoon it out of the liquid with a fine-mesh sieve. Keep it in a small bowl in the freezer until ready to use.

These techniques can also be successfully applied to savory dishes.

# Sodification

## *The Champagne of Techniques*

### About Carbonic Acid

In the world of gases, carbonic acid is only mentioned if it is dissolved in water. Up to that point it is called carbon dioxide: $CO_2$. You probably learned at school that many substances could exist in three states: gas, liquid and solids. However, carbon dioxide is an exception, it transforms from a solid to gas with no liquid state in between. In the 1980's scientists discovered that there is also a liquid form, but only under

certain pressure and temperature. Today fast food restaurants and nightclubs regularly use 180-liter cylinders of carbonic acid for their operations. While carbonic acid is a simple substance, you can still see three states in action: in a charger under pressure it is liquid; as you discharge the liquid, part of it becomes snow, while the other part can become gas. Caution: carbonic acid is poisonous and can cause paralysis. Treat it with respect.

José Andres is a disciple of Ferran Adrià and is a culinary phenomenon in the Washington, DC area. Andres demonstrated a carbonic acid technique during the gastronomic congress Lo major de la Gastronomia in San Sebastian, Spain. We have translated his imaginary name for the process into Sodification. His creation of oysters and champagne grapes was very impressive so we did some research ourselves. The principle of Sodification is very simple. The key is the basic preparation.

## Basic Preparation

*Ingredients:* 300 g seedless Muscat grapes, 30 g water, 1 soda charger ($CO_2$).

Cut the grapes off the stem and wash them thoroughly. Half fill a siphon with the wet grapes. Fill one-tenth of the total volume of the siphon with water and close. Insert the charger and refrigerate for at least six hours. In the siphon, the carbon dioxide fills the grapes with small bubbles that explode in your mouth when you eat them, providing an amazing experience. Fully discharge the soda from the siphon, remove the cap, take the grapes out and serve immediately. When you practice this, you will notice that the time to develop bubbles in the grapes will vary.

## Grapes Kir Royal

**Ingredients:** 200 g seedless white grapes, 50 g white wine,
20 g Crème de Cassis, 1 charger.

In this recipe you mix the grapes with the white wine and crème de
cassis instead of water. Fill the siphon and do the same as above.
Serve a small layer of grapes in a deep glass and pour some of the
juice over it.

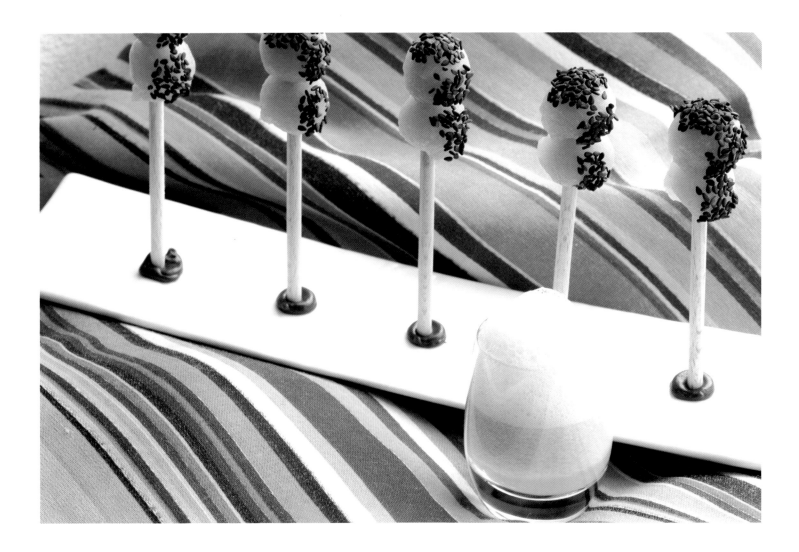

## Melon Fizz with white port

**Ingredients:** 30 small scooped melon balls, white port, black sesame seeds.

Mix the melon balls with the port, put in a siphon of half a liter and insert one charger. Let stand for a minimum of 6 hours. Discharge the liquid from the siphon, then remove the melon balls. Put toothpicks on the melon balls and lightly coat with the black sesame seed. Mix and bind the juice with a stick mixer and serve separately.

## Espresso jelly with spicy warm chocolate mousse

*For 10 glasses:* 500 g espresso coffee, 4 sheets of gelatin.
*For the mousse:* 200 g white chocolate, 200 g unsweetened whipping cream, 150 g pasteurized egg white, 1 soda charger.

Dissolve gelatin in warm water before adding it to the freshly made espresso coffee. Divide the jelly evenly in the glasses. Heat the whipping cream and dissolve the white chocolate in the warm whipping cream. Let cool and then add the egg white. Put the mixture in the siphon and insert the charger. Keep the siphon warm at 65°C/150°F. Spout the mousse on top of the jelly immediately.

These are just the first results of our experiments with this technique, so the times indicated in the recipes may vary. For example, there was very little effect to the grapes in less than three hours. But after sixteen hours the grapes were perfect, just as those we saw José Andres demonstrate. We are still working with these methods to find out which other products we can use with carbonic acid. We feel that products with a peel and a small opening are the most suitable. Most likely cherry tomatoes would also be very good to use. Raspberries, strawberries and blackberries become purée in the siphon. Solid fruit without a peel, such as melon balls, are also very suitable. We are even thinking of cucumber and continue to experiment. We would love to hear about your experiences, as together we can optimize this technique.

# New Chocolate
# structures

These are some spectacular chocolate applications for which you don't need years of experience as a chocolate expert to get the best result. All preparations can be made ahead and require very little planning.
The coral structure and the spun chocolate, for example, are very suitable as a finishing touch for pastry and cakes.

### Very thin caramel of chocolate

*Ingredients:* 90 g fondant, 40 g glucose, 40 g chocolate couverture (your choice of dark, milk or white).

Combine the glucose and fondant and bring to 155°C/310°F, take off the heat and let cool to 130°C/265°F. Add the chopped chocolate couverture and stir until smooth. Immediately pour the mixture on a silpat, cover with a second silpat and roll out to layer 5 millimeters thick. Let cool thoroughly, break into pieces and store in an airtight container. You can make the chocolate layer even thinner by putting it back in the oven between the 2 silpats at 160oC/320oF to soften it more and then roll it out again. Cool again and store in a covered container with a silica package to keep dry.

*Ingredients:* 200 g bitter chocolate couverture,
150 g unsweetened whipping cream, 150 g unpasteurized
egg white, 1 charger.

Bring the whipping cream to a boil, take off the stove and melt the chocolate in the cream. When the temperature is down to 60°C/140°F stir in
the egg white. Pour mixture in the siphon and insert the charger. Shake
the canister and keep it warm (70°C/160°F) in a Bain Marie. Shake the
canister again before use. Immediately dispense the warm foam on a
dessert with different chocolate structures or on a vanilla parfait.

This is a very simple way to make spectacular chocolate garnishes. It is prepared with dry ice, which will turn into gas within a limited time, so make many garnishes at once. The garnishes keep well in a dry and cool place.

Melt chocolate and bring to appropriate temperature. Put dry ice in a bowl. Pour chocolate in a piping bag or small cornet and create several little forms or shapes on the dry ice. Wait a few seconds until they have hardened and take them carefully off the ice (to avoid burns to your hands use latex gloves). Keep the coral in an airtight container at room temperature with a packet of silicone grains.

Pour 92% alcohol in a small container and put in the freezer for several hours or a whole day. The alcohol should be -18°C/0°F. Melt chocolate and pour into a piping bag or small cornet. Pour the chocolate rapidly in the alcohol and let harden for several seconds. Take the chocolate out of the alcohol and let the excess alcohol evaporate. Then store in an airtight container.

***Ingredients:*** 1000 g water, 400 g chocolate couverture (70%), 4 g soylecithin.

Cover a baking sheet with parchment paper and put in the freezer. Finely chop the chocolate, place in bowl and mix with the lecithin. Heat water to 90°C/195°F, then pour over the chocolate. Blend smooth with a hand-mixer and cool to 50°C/120°F. After it cools, use a mixer to make it very foamy and let rest for one minute to stabilize the foam. Pour into the prepared baking sheet and place in the freezer. Cover the baking sheet to avoid taste transfer and let freeze for another few hours. Take baking sheet out and invert contents onto an ice-cold plate and serve immediately. The foam will taste very cold at first, but then quickly melt, giving a very special taste to the palate.

# Old & New binding

## With classic gelatin and hyper-modern methyl cellulose

Chefs and pastry chefs are now inundated with new binding methods and techniques to change the structure of their products. Several of these products will earn a special place in the kitchen and others will disappear from the shelves of the stores within a year. So we thought it would be a great idea to outline a binding method that every chef already has in the kitchen and yet is a binding method not many people know about. We know the way gelatin works. But methyl cellulose can be used to bind or to gel and will dissolve in cold as well as hot water. It sets when hot and melts when cold! Methyl cellulose is sold under the name "Methyl" and a variety of textures. Just be aware that in this case the measurement of gelatin is extremely important. A sheet of gelatin does not always weigh exactly 2 g, which can give a totally different result.

### Marshmallows made of red beet

*Ingredients:* 150 g pureed red beets, 20 g gelatin powder, 500 g sugar, 240 g water, 60 g pasteurized egg white, dash of salt.

Mix the cold beet purée with the gelatin powder. Boil water and sugar to 125°C/260°F, take off the heat and add the purée when the water bubbles have disappeared. Mix well. Add a dash of salt to the egg whites and beat until they are stiff. Then add the hot beet purée in small drops to the mix. Mix for a bit longer and then cool. Dust a piece of parchment paper with icing sugar and squirt little drops of the mixture on top. Leave to dry for at least 3 hours at room temperature until it gets a little crust.

## Marshmallows "au gratin" with passion fruit

*Ingredients:* 250 g passion fruit coulis, 3.5 g methyl cellulose, 7 g gelatin.

On a small kitchen scale weigh exactly 3.5 g methyl cellulose and mix with 200 g of the coulis, using a hand-mixer. Put this mix in the refrigerator and let cool to 3°C/37°F. Stir regularly. The cooling is necessary to set the methyl cellulose. Take the mix out of the fridge and let warm to 14°C/60°F. Soak the gelatin in cold water. Heat the rest of the coulis to 50°C/120°F and dissolve the gelatin in it. Whisk the mixture with the methyl cellulose in a stand mixer and add the gelatin mix until it starts to bind lightly. Whisk for another 7 minutes until you get a very fluffy meringue. Pipe directly on the plate or silicone paper. Let rest for a few hours in the fridge and heat "au gratin" under a salamander. Suggestion: serve marshmallows in a small concoction of pure chocolate and coconut.

### Coffee "biscuit"

*Ingredients:* 360 g espresso, 120 g water, 8 g of gelatin (sheets).

Mix 70 g of water with the espresso. Put in the freezer and let cool to 1°C/34°F. Heat the rest of the water and dissolve the soaked gelatin in it. Beat this with a mixer to drastically increase the volume. Add the espresso mix a little bit at a time and keep beating until volume has increased five times from the start. Immediately put in an ice-cold bin to a depth of about 2 cm. Cover with aluminum foil and put in the freezer. Once frozen, cut into small squares and serve as a bottom layer for a dessert.

### "Solero" jelly

*Ingredients:* 500 g mango purée, 120 g glucose, 4 g of gelatin sheets, soaked in water.

This frozen fruit jelly will never become hard because of the glucose content, which gives it a certain melting pattern. This will remind you of the fruit jelly around a Solero ice cream. Heat 100 g mango purée with the glucose to 80°C/176°F and dissolve the pre-soaked gelatin in it. Mix with the rest of the purée. You now can work with this purée in different ways: just as a jelly, on or around an ice-cream dessert, or as a separate frozen layer of jelly. Cover an appropriate plate with plastic wrap, put a thin layer (3-4 mm) of mango purée on top and put in the freezer. On one of the photos you will notice a lollipop made of this recipe.

### Consommé of bitter chocolate with yogurt vermicelli

*For the consommé:* 1 ltr water, 200 g bitter chocolate,
6 g of gelatin (sheets), 50 g egg white.
*For the vermicelli:* 350 g yogurt, 150 g water, 7.5 g methyl cellulose.

For the consommé, heat water to 70°C/160°F, add the chocolate, mix well, and add the pre-soaked gelatin. Pour into a fitted container, cover and leave in the freezer for 12 hours. Let thaw and wait until the chocolate gets separated from the liquid. Strain the liquid through sieve. Put the egg white in the bottom of a pan, pour the chocolate bouillon on top and heat slowly until the egg white sets and comes to the top. Strain through a fine-mesh sieve with cheesecloth. Keep the clear consommé refrigerated until use. For the vermicelli, heat water to 85°C/185°F, add the methyl cellulose and dissolve well. Add the yogurt and place in the fridge. The yogurt will thicken in the hot liquid and become vermicelli. This effect is spectacular if you use it for a dinner setting. For this, heat the consommé to 80°C/175°F, pour in a warm glass and at the dinner table pipe fine threads of yogurt in the glass. The yogurt will immediately take shape and keep its form.

# *crunch and munch*

You can turn liquid into a crunchy substance with liquid nitrogen *(see warning on page 31)*. The technique allows us to create surprising contrasts in a dish, differences in structure and temperature that will give a normal taste combination an enormous sensation. We use two methods to create a crunchy cream. One is an edible dish in itself; the other is a crunchy layer around a liqueur.

## *Egg shells made of crunchy cream*

*Ingredients:* **liquid nitrogen, one dewar-vat (a double-insulated stainless steel bowl) oval spoon of your choice, digital alarm clock with the capability to measure seconds, 2 nesting bowls.**

The working method has to be very precise, but once you have it under control, you will be able to make lots of this. Fill a bowl with cold water and another bowl with (sweetened) whipping cream. Wet the oval spoon in water, then put it in the liquid nitrogen and wait until the surface of the liquid becomes smooth. Take the spoon out of the nitrogen and let rest on a table for exactly 30 seconds, using the digital alarm clock. Immerse the spoon with the curved side in the cream and then in the nitrogen. Hold it in there for 10 seconds and repeat it once more in the cream. Hold the spoon another 5 seconds in the liquid nitrogen. If you

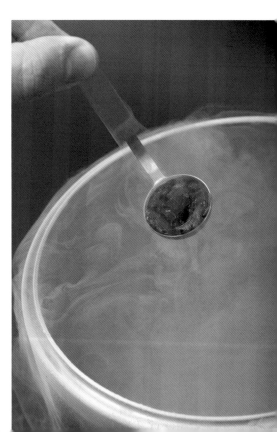

follow these instructions precisely, you will see that the crunchy cream loosens itself from the spoon. Put this immediately in a tight container in the freezer and leave it there for a minimum of 1 hour. They will keep very well in the freezer.

## Liqueur shots in crunchy cream

*Ingredients:* liquid nitrogen, dewar-vat, measuring spoons of 5 ml, perforated spoons, 1 plastic syringe, 2 small ramekins, 1 plastic slotted spoon.

Bend the spoons so that the stem of the spoon is perpendicular to the bowl. Fill one ramekin with the sweetened cream and the other one with a layer of liqueur of your choice. Fill the syringe with the liqueur. Hold the curved spoon in the nitrogen until the surface of the nitrogen comes to a rest. Take the spoon out of the liquid, squirt the liqueur into the spoon, submerge it again and freeze thoroughly. The small little ball that has now been formed will come off very easily. It is crucial that the spoon is first ice cold; otherwise the liqueur will not come off. Drop the little ball in the sweetened cream and take it out after 3 seconds with the perforated spoon. Drop it again in the nitrogen and take it out after a few seconds with the plastic slotted spoon. Use the plastic spoon because the ball will roll off more easily than with a metal spoon. Submerge the little ball "bonbon" once again in the cream and let harden for a few more seconds. Leave the bonbons in the freezer for at least one hour at -18°C/0°F). The cream will stay crunchy at this temperature, while the liqueur becomes fluid again.

 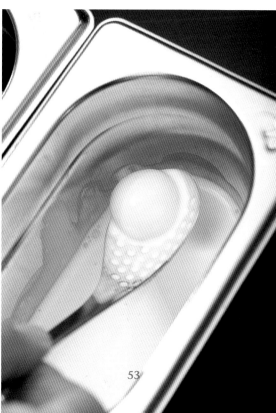 

### Crunchy Cream with Tia Maria
Use unsweetened cream and Tia Maria.

### Vanilla cream with wild strawberry liqueur
Make vanilla cream by using a sliced vanilla bean simmered in part of the cream. Then mix the vanilla cream with the rest of the cream and make liqueur shots with the liqueur.

### Coconut cream with chocolate liqueur
Mix coconut cream with sweetened whipping cream and create liqueur shots with the chocolate liqueur.

### Crunchy cream with peach liqueur
Use unsweetened cream because of the sweetness of the liqueur.

### Pistachio cream with raspberry liqueur
Grind 100 g green pistachios and 300 ml sweetened cream in a blender and pour through a fine-mesh sieve. Mix together with the raspberry liqueur for the liqueur shots.

### Structures of Irish Coffee
*Ingredients:* 200 ml unsweetened whipping cream, 300 ml espresso coffee, 80 g sugar water (1:1), 75 g brown sugar, 35 g water, 35 g Irish whiskey, cocoa powder.

Mix the espresso with the sugar water, put in the freezer, and stir regularly with a fork so you get a fine granita. Make a crunchy cream eggshell as described previously and put in the freezer until they have reached the right consistency. Mix water and brown sugar and boil until it becomes a light syrup. Add the whiskey and cook a bit more. Pour some of the granita in a soup plate, put the crunchy eggshell on top, sprinkle with a bit of cocoa powder and serve immediately. At the dinner table pour the brown sugar syrup on top, so that the flavours get mixed, but the structure stays the same.

D09

## Pina Colada Eggs

*Ingredients:* 100 ml sweetened whipping cream, 100 ml coconut milk, 300 g pineapple coulis, 100 g sugar water (1:1), 100 g dark rum, liquid nitrogen.

Mix the whipping cream and the coconut milk together and make half-size crunchy shells. Put the pineapple coulis in a heavy metal bowl and mix with liquid nitrogen until you get a smooth sorbet. Heat the rum and the sugar water to a boiling point and pour in a little china jug. Fill the crunchy cream shell with the sorbet and cover with the other half of the shell, so you get a beautiful kind of cone. Put this in a small dish and pour the hot syrup on top while you are at the dinner table, so that the content becomes visible.

## Kinder Eggs

This is an egg shell of bitter chocolate and crunchy cream with sorbet made of pistachio nuts and chocolate kadaïf (a Turkish stringy dough). This is a cute twist on the popular children's treat, Kinder Egg, because of its form and radiance.

*Ingredients:* 100 ml sweetened whipping cream, 100 g pure chocolate, 50 g cocoa butter, 125 g peeled pistachios, 150 g water, stringy dough, 100 g couverture chocolate, 100 g unsalted butter, sugar water.

Make an eggshell of the whipping cream as described in previous recipes. Melt the chocolate and the cocoa butter together. Immerse the chilled eggshell in the melted mixture and freeze. Puree the pistachio nuts with water and sugar water, then pour through a fine-mesh sieve in frix beakers and freeze to -20°C/-4°F. Immediately use a Frix Air machine to make the pistachio mixture into a sorbet.
Melt the couverture with the butter and mix very carefully with the kadaïf dough, so that all strings are coated with a thin layer. Create very fluffy little balls and bake in the oven for 5 minutes at 200°C/390°F until they are crunchy. Take the eggshell out of the freezer, put a quenelle of pistachio sorbet in the shell and finish with a small ball of chocolate kadaïf.

## Eggs Romanov

Make an eggshell of sweet cream as described previously. Cut strawberries in brunoise and mix with Grand Marnier. Spoon this in the eggshells and finish with a quenelle of strawberry sorbet and yogurt streusel (streusel that is made with yogurt powder).

Over the years he has won many awards and prizes and although many see him as the best and most modern pâtissier in Belgium, he sees it differently: "You know, there is a major difference between restaurant pâtissiers and confisseurs. Having a restaurant gives you more opportunities to think out of the box, the media comes to you. It is much more difficult for a confisseur. I was lucky with the media, the reason why I was called the best very quickly. But I don't see myself that way at all. Innovative, yes, I would say so. With my new ideas of presentations I hope to get people thinking."

# The inspiration
## Roger van Damme

## Explosive

"Pâtisserie has to get a new approach," Roger says. "By using a whole new structure of food, I can see and use products totally differently. Each item on a dish will be individually presented. If you eat things separately, you can get a much stronger taste. But what is important for me, is that everything I present has the same structure." All crèmes have the same texture, the crunchy items have a different taste, but still the same interpretation and bite. This way you won't get confused by a lot of differences and you can concentrate on the taste. "Who says that pâtisserie has to be the way it is? Why do we have to present everything as a little tart or prepare it as a mousse or a bavarois? The taste sensation in your mouth is all that counts. Because of the individual items, the guest can make the combination himself. It will all come to an explosion in the mouth!" It is characteristic for Roger that none of his dishes are excessive: "A dish should carry its own decoration." Roger has repeated it a few times: for him structure is the most important. "I use the thermo mixer a lot. This makes it more refined, and enhances the taste. It is Gunther Van Essche from pâtisserie Del Rey, who takes it even further when it comes to structure. I see him as the best pâtissier of Belgium. He has one disadvantage, his creations have to be sold as separate items

and have to be kept well in the showcase. I have more possibilities as I present everything on a plate. Therefore I can use dry ingredients. But his structures are an inspiration for me." Everything on the plate has to have a function, and correlate with the dish. The new way of presenting doesn't have to be a mint leaf or a raspberry. "I do what I like. The guest is not totally ready for this approach. I can use it as part of a menu, but not as a separate item with coffee. That doesn't work."

## Modesty

What we have noticed before and even today, is the fact that Roger presents himself in a very modest and open way. No hint of arrogance here. "In Holland I won the dessert trophy of the year and last year my dessert menu was chosen as the best of the country. This is the reason why I have to keep coming up with new ideas. However, I am not alone and am very open with my colleagues. I have a number of people who I help behind the scenes and also people who inspire and help me. Together we can create new and beautiful concepts." His greatest inspiration? He already mentioned Gunter Van Essche but second is Alberto Adrià, the reason why Roger often travels to Spain. But that doesn't mean he copies these inspiring colleagues. "I use the inspiration to develop my own style. Of course, I was very lucky that I was an apprentice at El Bulli and that our relationship there is superb. Therefore we already had melon caviar many years ago. However, I don't see Spain as sacred, I only use 10% of it on my menu. I do read an awful lot and use what is relevant. Since I am very involved in photography, I approach my desserts differently which has led to new trends." Roger would like to see higher standards in pâtisserie. "There is not a country in the world that has seen so much evolution in pâtisserie as Belgium. There are many top pâtissiers in our country, who are better than me, they just were not so lucky getting publicity."

www.hetgebaar.be

D09

# Brown

### *Crunchy Chocolate*

*Ingredients:* 500 g fondant, 250 g glucose, 250 g isomalt, 100 g cocoa powder.

Mix 100 g fondant with the glucose, heat to 160°C/320°F; add isomalt and the rest of the fondant and heat to 140°C/285°F. Add the cocoa powder, cool and grind to a powder in the thermo mixer. Sprinkle the powder on a silpat and bake in a pre-heated oven at 170°C/338°F for 80 seconds. Take out of the oven and let sit until it becomes crunchy and break it in pieces. This crunch is extremely well suited to garnish desserts.

### *Cocoa Powder*

*Ingredients:* 80 g dark chocolate, 30 g cocoa powder, 30 g sugar, 100 g cream, 300 g water.

Mix the cocoa powder with the sugar and mix the cream with the water. Combine both mixtures together, bring to a boil and dissolve the chocolate in it. Put in a Frix beaker and freeze. Swirl the powder around when necessary and keep in the freezer. This powder can serve as a nice gadget on a dessert or part of a dessert. For example, El Bulli serves this powder as a combination with lime and wasabi. Once it has had enough twirls, simply keep it in the freezer.

## Yellow

### Mango yolk

*Ingredients:* 1 liter mangopuree, 8 g algin, 1 litre water, 5 g calcic.

Using a hand blender, mix part of the puree with the algin. Add the rest
of the puree and mix well. Mix the water with the calcic. Using a ladle,
spoon the mango puree in the calcium bath. Leave the yolk in there for
160 seconds and then rinse with clear water. This "yolk" technique is
often copied. Roger shows us how it really should be done. It is important
to know that not every coulis can be used for this. It is extremely
important to know the degree of acidity. The coulis should also not be
too thin. Therefore Roger always uses coulis of Boiron that meets all the
requirements. The yolk can be seen as a liquid jelly on a tart for instance.
There will be a lot more of these applications in the future.

## Mango crunch

*Ingredients:* 450 g mango puree, 120 g icing sugar,
75 g isomaltose, 15 g glucose.

Mix all the ingredients in a thermo mixer of 80°C/175°F. Spread the
mixture on a silpat and bake at 120°C/250°F for 100 seconds. This again
is a garnish. The crunch is best kept in a dry and cool place. To avoid
stickiness, it is advisable to put a little box of silica-gel in the container.
This absorbs any moisture.

# White

### *Cellophane of sugar*

Heat sugar pearls to 160°C/320°F and cool a bit. Dip a small iron pipe in the sugar pearls and blow thin cellophane out of it. With some practice it will be possible to use this technique for wrapping products in "cellophane". Make sure that the products don't contain a lot of moisture. For example, you can use it to wrap nuts.

### *Sugar pastilles*

*Ingredients:* **sugar pearls, hazelnut oil, plastic pipettes.**

Heat the sugar pearls to 160°C/320°F and let cool. Suck the hazelnut oil up in the pipette and form a little ball of sugar around it. Squeeze the oil into the sugar and pinch it carefully so the pastille will close. This application is ideal to give an extra boost of taste to a dish. You can also use other oils, but no liquids to do this.

*Cressperience*

# Koppert Cress

**You can find these flavourful miniature plants in every star restaurant in Europe and now they are also known in the United States.**

Rob Baan used to work in a seed growing company and was always looking for unique and unknown plants throughout the world. The tropical rain forests and the far removed Asian regions were a particular part of his work. He observed the behaviour of primitive people and discovered that they were often collecting young plant sprouts. He brought the most flavourful ones to Europe and started cultivating these himself.

In 2002, Rob took over the company, called it Koppert Cress and went his own new direction. For the marketing he focused totally on the chefs and not on the commercial companies. He felt the chefs were interested, the companies would follow. Rob was right. You can see these miniplants in restaurant kitchens all over Europe. The demand was also growing in America so he opened a production company in the United

States.

## The Taste Garden

Rob's company is in Holland, between the cities of The Hague and Rotterdam, where he has an extensive greenhouse complex and a distribution center. Then there is also the Cressperience, a professional test kitchen, a meeting place for chefs from every country. The greenhouse complex is one of the most modern in the world with a fully automatic system. The cleaned seeds go directly into a prepared package and are then moved to an assigned spot in the greenhouse. Millions of these grow in a clean environment at the right temperature and humidity; during the day they get sunlight and at night artificial light. When the little plants are ready they are transported to the distribution centre by a small electric train.

One part of the greenhouse complex is made into a tasting garden. Here we saw several plants we had never seen before, mostly from tropical countries. Sometimes Koppert Cress discovers amazing flavours already used for consumption in exotic places. Biologists then research and test for the most optimal production and storage conditions. Every year new kinds of cress or other specialties hit the market and each time we are amazed again.

## Chefs

Rob is extremely inspired by chefs who know how to use his products the right way. That is why he had a large professional kitchen built next to his greenhouses. Cressperience is the envy of many chefs. In the middle of this kitchen sits a large oval Molteni stove. It is a unique stove because only three have ever been built. Chefs from many countries come together in the Cressperience-kitchen to develop new ideas. In the adjacent greenhouses they can pick any fresh cress they desire. Rob likes to introduce his visiting chefs to the gardeners who live in the neighbourhood. Rob: "Gardeners and chefs can learn a lot from each other and there should be chemistry between them. Chefs are an inspiration in developing products and flavours."

One of the people Rob works with is the Spanish three star chef Ferran Adriá, who has the most innovative kitchen in the world. Every time Rob discovers a new little plant, Ferran Adriá will experiment with it. His brother Alberto Adriá does the same in pâtisserie. You will often see a new product of Koppert Cress in the latest creations that are shown every year by the brothers Adriá. Rob has a lot of respect for the Spanish chefs and pâtissiers: "They really draw the flavour out of every product, often with simple techniques. They see the kinds of cress not as a garnish but more as an intense taste factor."

## Health

Besides the strong flavour, cress also has many healthy and protective qualities. Of course for a chef taste is the most important, because the restaurant guests are primarily there to enjoy themselves. But when this enjoyment can be combined with health, it's a win-win situation. Rob: "Very young plants, like cress, contain many protective substances. A small plant that starts to germinate is exposed to many dangers of the bad world and is guarded against it. Just look at the animals in nature, they will always go for young sprouts." Humans can take advantage of these protective substances and many Koppert Cress products have a high concentration in them.

## America

As mentioned, the demand in the States for products of Koppert Cress has become spectacular. Sending daily Trans-Atlantic air shipments to the importer Coosemans New York was not very practical. So in 2006 the companies Koppert Cress and Coosemans decided to start cultivating the plants in America. Rob Baan: "We started to look for a location with the same climate as Holland and found this on Long Island. After the second World War a number of Dutch farmers came to the area and through them we found the right spot on the North Fork of Long Island." The sea climate on Long Island has the characteristics of temperate summers and mild winters. Rob Baan finds Long Island the ideal place to work. "We are close to Manhattan and right between the wine growers. I deliberately wanted to set up a company on the East Coast, this spot is a culinary Mecca."

Because of its previous export experience, the company knows what the clients want and the variety is adapted accordingly. Now, each chef in North America can order his products from his own country and products can be delivered as fresh as possible because of a good transportation method. In America, Rob Baan has given the responsibilities to Nicolas Mazard and Eddy Creces, who are in charge of the company on Long Island. Should you not live in Europe or in North America, you can still get this remarkable cress because the mini-plants are exported worldwide. Anywhere in the world you will find Dutch exporters, talk to them and they will make sure you receive these special products and flavours. Or check the website for sales addresses. Here is a summary of the varieties of Koppert Cress, with a small description of flavours and applications.

Koppert Cress Europe
De Poel 1 – Monster (The Netherlands)
Phone: +31-174 24 28 19

Koppert Cress USA LLC
22425 Middle Road/Route 48
Cutchogue NY 11935
Phone: +1 516 437 57 00

## Affilla Cress [1]

This variety comes from South-East Asia, where this real snow pea has a luxurious and radiant appearance. It has the flavour of fresh and raw peas but it is not dominant. It is well suited for bouillons and garnishes.

## Apple Blossom [2]

This decorative heart and angel shaped little flower with a salmon colour has the distinctive taste of a green apple. Very suitable for a variety of desserts and cocktails. Because of the colour the guests have a totally different taste association.

## Atsina Cress [3]

Has a very aromatic sweet flavour that is like licorice. Endless combinations with desserts are possible. It beats the peppermint leaf not only in presentation but also in digestion. A new product that promises a lot for the future.

## Basil Cress [4]

This is the real sweet basil. The entire plant can be used, unlike the big bunches of basil that must be stemmed. It gives an inspiring basil flavour to pesto.

## Borage Cress [5]

A light briny flavour with a bit of iodine. It has also a flavour of fresh cucumber, even an oyster. Combines very well with fish.

## BroccoCress® [6]

Has a very healthy cabbage taste and has, in comparison with broccoli, a high content of healthy substances. Contains many anti-oxidants. Should be eaten raw.

## Daikon Cress [7]

Daikon is a radish kind of root. The Japanese name is Kaiware. It has a strong radish taste and goes well with sushi, but is also very suitable with fish and meat.

## Ghoa Cress [8]

Derived its name from a region in India where it is used in many dishes. A fresh citrus flavour and mild aroma of coriander. Of course, the seeds go very well with Asian dishes, even with desserts. The leaves are very decorative.

## Karma Orchid [9]

This orchid is specially cultivated for Koppert Cress in Thailand and in the Netherlands. It has a fresh and neutral taste, comparable to Boston lettuce and Belgian endive. The orchids have been thoroughly tested and are fully edible and can be used as decoration as well.

## Limon Cress [10]

Is one of the 150 edible basil varieties. In the taste that lingers on for some time the lime comes to the surface and changes to mint. In the back of the throat it tastes like pastis. Easy to combine with desserts, but also with oysters, mussels and salmon.

## Mustard Cress [11]

This cress has a nutty taste that is quick and strong, just like wasabi with sushi. Yet it is a mustard cress. It gives just the right amount of aroma that you might need in a dish.

## Oyster Leaves [12]

Have a bit of a briny flavour and reminds you of oysters and are sometimes called vegetarian oysters. They are an interesting addition in combination with seafood and other ingredients.

## Rock Chives® [13]

This kind of Chinese leek grows, as the name says, in a rocky area. It has a striking appearance with thin small stalks and little black buttons. You don't taste the leek flavour in the front of the mouth but in the back where it is nice and smooth. It doesn't exude a smell, like garlic.

## Rucola Cress [14]

The little brother of the well-known salad leaves. A nice nutty taste, that gives a strong peppery taste in the throat.

## Sakura® Cress [15]

The purple variety of the Daikon Cress, but less flavourful. The leaves are very decorative and healthy. They contain autocyan, a red colouring that is good for heart and blood vessels.

## Salicornia Cress [16]

This cress has a mild salty taste with a crunchy bite, ideal for fish recipes. It is a young plant and comes from the popular sea asparagus. It is available all year, can be used entirely and does not have to be cleaned.

## Sechuan Buttons [17]

The flower comes from the Chinese province with the same name and gives, if used in food, the same taste as Szechuan pepper, although there is no relation. The little flower heads are mainly used for the "electric" effect that takes place in the mouth. It starts with a sparkling effect on the tip of the tongue but then changes to a tingling and an anesthetic sensation of the cheeks and the entire tongue, which creates a lot of saliva. A very different experience to wake up your guests! That is the way Ferran Adriá sees it.

## Sechuan Cress [18]

Gives a very surprising taste that is tingling, peppery and lively. First impression is green and young, later it becomes stimulating. Gives a surprising effect in amuses.

## Shiso Green [19]

A traditional Japanese product. First it gives a mint taste in the front of the mouth, whereas it has an anise taste in the back of the mouth. Can easily replace the century old mint leaf because it is easily digested and has a nice flavour.

## Shiso® Purple [20]

The large leaves are a traditional Japanese product. They are very aromatic and full of flavour that reminds you of cumin.

## Shiso Leaves [21]

Available in a red and green variety. A very traditional product in the Japanese kitchen, called Oba, especially when green leaves are used in combination with raw fish. Has a cleansing effect and a strong taste. Can be used as a serious herb in dishes. The taste is stronger than in the cress not only in the mouth but also in the nose.

## Tahoon® Cress [22]

These are the shoots of an Asian tree. The nutty taste reminds you of burnt beech nuts, giving you an autumn feeling. Goes very well with game, and very well with goat cheese and honey.

## Venus Vase [23]

The Venus Vase is a natural "glass" that would impress and surprise your guests in a creative and unique way. Use as an aperitif or a provocative cocktail. Although the Venus Vase is not edible, it can be used without any problems for serving drinks. The glass is so strong that it can be washed several times with lukewarm water. The Venus vase belongs to a group of plant cups that you see especially in the rain forests of South East Asia. The plant feeds on insects because it excretes special nectar that draws the insects to them. The glass is strong and suitable for alcoholic and non-alcoholic drinks.

## Wheat Grass [24]

Wheat grass has to be juiced. The juice gives a sweet and intensive flavour that will remind you of grass. The colour is very deep and contains minerals.

13

14

15

16

17

18

19

20

21

22

23

24

## Duo of Atsina coffee delicacies
### After Eight and mandarin Atsina cocktail

*For the After Eight:* 200 g tempered white chocolate, 1 small bowl of Atsina Cress.
*For the cocktail:* 1 small bowl of Atsina Cress, 200 ml mandarin juice, 100 ml Malibu rum, marrow of 1/2 vanilla bean, 100 ml coconut milk.

For the After Eight, pick leaves of Atsina Cress and put on a sheet of polypropylene. Using a cornet, pipe dots of tempered white chocolate on the cress leaves and cover with another sheet of polypropylene. Put skewers in the dots and let the chocolate harden. For the cocktail, heat the mandarin juice with the vanilla marrow, cool and divide over the glasses. Carefully pour the Malibu on the juice. Foam coconut milk with a hand blender and spoon on the cocktail. Garnish with an After Eight and a small leaf of Atsina.

## Carpaccio of mango with Atsina oil, peanuts and pink pepper syrup

*For the carpaccio:* 1 mango, 50 roasted peanuts.
*For the oil:* 200 ml peanut oil, 1 small bowl of Atsina Cress.
*For the red pepper syrup:* 200 ml mango coulis, 5 g pink pepper corns, 70 g sugar.

For the carpaccio, slice mango in very thin slices. For the oil, divide Atsina Cress over a Frix beaker and fill with oil to the indicated fill line. Freeze and Frix before use. For the pink pepper syrup cook the mango coulis with ground pink pepper corns, and the sugar to a syrup. Place thin slices of mango neatly on a plate and drizzle the sauce and oil on it. Garnish with peanuts and a leaf of Atsina Cress.

### Tapioca of almond milk with Atsina jelly and Atsina ice cream

*For the tapioca:* 40 g tapioca, 200 g burnt almonds, 2 litres milk, sugar.

*For the Atsina jelly:* 200 ml white wine, 2 small bowls of chopped Atsina Cress, 50 g sugar, 3 sheets of gelatin.

*For the Atsina ice cream:* 375 g cream, 270 g milk, 38 g sugar, 150 g egg yolks, 110 g sugar, 2 small bowls of Atsina Cress.

*For the crumble:* 100 g flour, 100 g cold butter, 100 g fine white sugar, 100 g almond powder.

For the tapioca, heat milk with the almonds and let simmer for one hour. Strain the milk and cook the tapioca slowly in the milk until done, strain and add sugar to taste. For the jelly, heat the wine with the sugar and dissolve the pre-soaked gelatin in it. Chop the Atsina Cress and add when wine starts to gel. For the ice cream, cook cream, milk and 38 g sugar. Whip egg yolks with the rest of the sugar and prepare as an anglaise. Pour the cooled mixture in Frix beakers. Freeze for at least 10 hours at –20ºC/–4ºF. Divide half a bowl of Atsina Cress per beaker to add on the surface and put in Frix machine. For the crumble, knead flour, butter, sugar and almond powder to a coarse mixture. Bake crumble in the oven at 180ºC/355ºF till golden and cool. Spoon tapioca in a cocktail glass; pour a thin layer of jelly on top and place in the fridge. Serve with a layer of crumble and a quenelle of ice cream.

D09

# Los Postres de
# **Barcelona**

Time flies. Just twenty years ago Barcelona was still a poor provincial city. After the summer Olympics, it is a prosperous metropolitan city visited by millions of tourists every year. It is also booming in the pastry sector. We discovered that Barcelona has the world's most modern pâtissiers, chefs and chocolatiers...

It is the first day of spring when we settle into our lodgings close to La Rambla, a long walkway that cuts through the booming heart of Barcelona. It's not hard to understand why the province of Catalonia has a great history in pâtisserie. The first chocolate imported to Europe from South America arrived here, and you can see the history everywhere. If you take the time and effort to stroll the labyrinth of streets behind La Rambla you will discover many small pastry shops. Definitely worthwhile is a little alley called Petritxol, where you will find the classic xocolateria. Drink (or better eat) a bitter chocomilk with unsweetened cream and dip a churro, coco or other Catalonian viennoiserie in it.

## Share with Friends

Before we took off for sunny Spain, we called our friend Santiago Rebés, a chef at the dessert restaurant EspaiSucre. Santi's girlfriend is Dutch and he also worked for many years in the Netherlands. His excellent Dutch language skills made our touring easy, especially since he offered to be our guide for a few days in sweet Barcelona and became our Catalan interpreter when necessary. It might be Italy that leads trends in fashion, but when it comes to pastry it is Barcelona where new ideas are born and sweet concepts developed. One custom became immediately clear: Tasting and sharing with friends are the key words for the future. The same counts for going back to the basics and the importance of taste.

Techniques have become secondary. We see it in every pastry shop: Small tables with a beautiful display of sweet and sparkling wines and a showcase of small pieces of pâtisserie. Sometimes the pastries are a bit bigger so they can be shared with friends. This is the same for the glasses found in each showcase, which are large enough for more than one person to share when eating.

It is impossible to visit all the pastry shops in Barcelona, so we restricted our choices to the largest ones in the city. If you can still manage to eat more after visiting these shops, and want further temptations and knowledge, we recommend a visit to Bubo, where chef Carlos Mampel reigns, you will find his shop just behind La Rambla and also find what pastry tasting really means! But, if you want to taste everything from bonbons, original chocolates and any other chocolate concoctions, head for Cacao Sampaka. Try the extreme bonbons with anchovies, Parmesan cheese, olive oil, black truffle or smoke. And don't forget to visit the biggest attraction of La Rambla: La Boqueria. This huge covered market is worth an entire day of visiting and eating. Vegetables and fruit, meat, charcuterie and hams, numerous fish stalls... However, we came for pâtisserie, and took in the stalls with magnificent displays of tropical fruits, nuts and the large assortment of candied fruit. You can't leave without a piece of fig tart or turron (nougat) to take home. Those are enough travel tips for now, on to the pâtissiers.

# Oriol Balaguer
## *The Designer*

Our first stop is with Oriol Balaguer. This pâtisserie-couturier is a long way from La Rambla in one of the more expensive neighbourhoods, and for good reason. At the age of 21 Oriol was already recognized as the best pâtissier of Spain. That achievement was just the start of a very impressive list of awards. Thirteen years later he is still considered as an innovator and trendsetter. We met him at his taller at the Carrer Morales. This is just his atelier or workshop, not his store. Oriol was working at Wittamer, discovered France, Madrid and Alicante, and worked seven years at El Bulli. "Before I started at El Bulli, I was only familiar with pâtisserie shops and suddenly I worked at a restaurant. This opened my eyes and widened my horizons." In 2002, Oriol opened his own business, a small shop with a big kitchen. Soon after that he opened a Japanese establishment, and a boutique in Barcelona. Today, his bonbons are exported all over Europe and are available in numerous specialty shops. Most pastry chefs know him because of his book, Dessert Cuisine, chosen as the best gastronomic book of the year in

2002. The book featured only creations we don't find at all in his shops. His specialty is chocolate, but he also fashions cakes and viennoiserie. Similar to a fashion king, Oriol develops four new collections of bonbons every year. All of them have the form of a cocoa bean; the only difference is on the outside through the colors and hand-painted motifs. The collections are named simply according to the number of different tastes: 12, 16, or 18. This spring we see jasmine tea, Pear William, cardamom, spices, whiskey, and peta feta (the famous little fizz balls). Besides this collection, we are totally overwhelmed by Collection Nippon, three Japanese flavours: wasabi, soy sauce and matcha tea. In spite of his enormous success, Oriol is a shy person. He would have us taste rather than have him talking a lot! We see a tart collection, and taste twelve different nuts that are presented as a truffle covered in chocolate. In the kitchen where at least 15 employees work daily, we see another specialty that attracts all of Barcelona to Oriol's shop: an enormous assortment of Easter eggs in incredible varieties. To understand his

Concept

El Paradigma

Escarchado

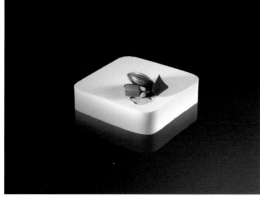

Exótico

Mágico

Collection Golf

philosophy better, we go quickly to his boutique. Our jaws drop when we enter his design shop, which reminds us of a jewelry store. Two Brazilian beauties welcome the customers. The store is not full; there is only one example of each product. We view a collection of six tarts. A special shelf is reserved for a new tart concept, which, if it is a success, will become part of the collection next year. We see many chocolates, viennoiserie, and wines to match; all presented in a framework of metal, mirrors and backlit walls. The collections are explained in a more comprehensive way on a built-in computer screen. We noticed in the showcase that most of the pâtisserie is displayed in glasses. Not just to eat, but to share with friends. We are impressed and this is just the first stop of our trip!

Magnum

Nins

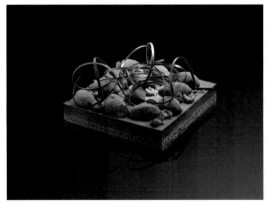

Nuestrosacher

Sidney

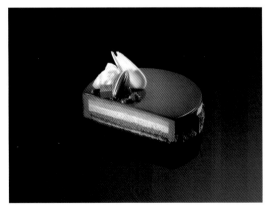

Tarragona

Tierra

## Christian Escriba
### *Dreams and Philosophy*

*"Have you ever seen a suitcase filled with $100,000?"* This is how our conversation starts with Señor Escriba. Then he shows us a large suitcase with chocolate money on the table. The tone for our conversation is set. This pâtisserie business has been in the family since 1906. Christian is the fourth generation, but he has completely changed course. When we enter the store, the atmosphere is rather traditional, but our perception changes drastically when Christian starts his story. For more than two hours we watch a large screen showing his work, but mostly his philosophy. Christian does not believe in traditions. What do you think of flying, explosive and dancing cakes? The people at Escriba create a wall, dress a beautiful lady, build a Formula-1 car from chocolate or meringue and fill it with hundreds of chocolate brochettes. The guests don't get a piece of cake, but can indulge in anything that comes on a small stick. This can range from chocolate to fruit, from sugar candy to bonbons and so on. It is hard to explain in words what the presentations look like. Walls of tens of square meters, real size cars, the possibilities are endless. And then we see cakes that are alive! Female dancers are dressed in sugar, festooned with brochettes. Actors, musicians and dancers accompany these cakes. What we find doubtful are the exploding cakes. A base of paper and meringue is presented with great ceremony, and then it explodes in the presence of the guests. Truly a spectacle, but that's not all. "My motto is that we want to be different. I am a dreamer, that's why you don't see me in a chef jacket. I would rather sit in an office to create ideas and be a philosopher. People always think that pâtisserie has to be big and lots.

That is the wrong thought, it should just take a bit of care and attention." Things appear on the table that we are not allowed to photograph. These are the first prototypes that undoubtedly will become world hits. A hotel doorknob with a little holder filled with bonbons. You can hang these at your girlfriend's door with a sweet message. Or a little chocolate ducky that you see in kid's swimming pools. This little ducky floats around in the coffee, starts sweating and a few seconds later immerses its little head in the coffee. And we haven't even told you about the message bears, sugar bears that you can give as presents to friends. Every bear carries another message.

What started as an over-the-top joke became Christian's big success. Once, he made a bride's dress completely of sugar. To complete the event he also created accessories out of sugar. That evening, every lady received an elaborate edible ring. This idea took off and was presented worldwide on a Valentine's Day. Harrods immediately put in an order and these rings are now available all over the world. Hundreds of different rings were created and this collection is now available in 22 different versions. On a metal changeable size ring, a form is attached of isomalt sugar, which has every possible flavour, form or colour. It is a very simple idea, but we have never seen it before. Moreover, for the price, you might consider buying a real silver ring!

Old machines from a marine ship were dressed in cheerful little coats. An Idea!

In Barcelona almost everything is on little sticks

# Jordi Butron

*Espai sucre*

The restaurant of Jordi Burton is like no other, something you would expect in a world city like Barcelona. The sweet dishes play the key factor here. Out of three menus, two are completely dedicated to desserts. The savoury dishes on the menu always include a technique from the patisserie or have a sweet accent. This can be a sorbet, a little tart, or a compôte of marmalade. "I don't allow myself to use savoury in my desserts, like garlic or fish. Even in pâtisserie, we have to look at principles and values, which we have to respect." When we ask Jordi who he really is, his answer is determined: "It is not who I am, it is the restaurant that counts. We are a dessert restaurant, attached to a school, which is totally dedicated to desserts. I started this simply because I love pâtisserie. The fact that I started a school is because I took courses about this at one time. You will never find just one flavour in my dishes, because we are always looking for a combination. You will often be intrigued by a dish, which will ask your full attention every time. They are simple but also complex. Simplicity can be very complex, and complexity can be very simple." We are in Barcelona, and the image we have is that everything has to do with techniques. "That is definitely not

The courses of Espai sucre are taught in a luxurious environment

the case with us, taste has to be all and foremost. The technique is a tool, but should never be the goal. I start with an ingredient and find the appropriate technique for it. You'll have to find the right combination of these two to get the desired result. Nowadays, it seems that it is all show and not taste." We enjoy this evening with a dinner that focuses our attention to extreme combinations in taste, which creates many discussions at our table. The hearty garlic soup with mussels, poached duck egg and a thin crêpe with saffron, make us delirious. The five bitter tastes in the dessert of beer, chicory, yogurt, walnut and cruesli are almost hard to understand. Not everyone would appreciate this. From all over Europe, particularly South America, students come to Barcelona to take courses from Jordi. The waiting lists are long, as only 14 students can be enrolled in the program at the same time. The courses teach only restaurant pâtisserie. The eleven-month course teaches practical as well as theoretical content with great emphasis on the product. Besides this intensive program, the school offers a one-time course on Mondays, which is available to anyone, on various subjects and guest chefs. Ferran and Albert Adrià are regulars there.

# Santiago Rebés Weindl

We met him by accident on one of our trips to Barcelona, but after an extensive exploration of this Spanish city, we can surely call him a very good friend. He was our interpreter during the very difficult Catalonian discussions and showed us the most beautiful spots and the best addresses in Catalonia. We will visit him again soon to learn more about trendy Barcelona. Santi has had a Dutch girlfriend for more than ten years, which prompted his chef years ago to ask him to go to the Netherlands for a demonstration; after all he knew the language. However, the harsh northern climate convinced him to return to Barcelona, the city where he grew up. He studied at the school of Jordi Butron and when finished he was asked to stay on, a challenge he could not refuse. "I have been here for a few years and finally begin to understand the style of Jordi. He is one of the few in the world who has entirely his own style that is hard to get into. Combinations of tradition and modernism, complex and simple, savoury and sweet, it is hard to get." Classic desserts are getting a new look and are totally rebuilt. "We have a concept here that will only work in the metropolitan cities like New York and Los Angeles. I would love to have my own business but then a normal one. But my love for combining sweet and savoury flavours comes from Jordi."

**www.espaisucre.com**

## Mango tart with thyme and pineapple sorbet

*For the mango tart:* 315 g yogurt, 125 g sugar, 250 g manchego cheese (Spanish sheep cheese) 65 g milk, 38 g corn starch, 18 g flour, 4 eggs, 200 g pineapple, 20 g butter, 20 g sugar.
*For the thyme sablé:* 500 g flour, 350 g butter, 250 g sugar, 10 g salt, 8 g ground thyme, 90 g egg yolks.
*For the pineapple marinade:* 600 g sugar water 1:1, 200 g water, 60 g Pernod.
*For the thyme parfait:* 300 g egg yolk, 225 g sugar, 200 g cream, 30 g dried thyme, 6 sheets of gelatin, 800 g fluffy whipped cream.
*For the pineapple sorbet:* 2 kg pineapple coulis, 170 g glucose, 80 g invert sugar, 200 g pineapple juice, 50 g rum, 7 g sorbet stabilizer.

For the tart caramelize cubes of pineapple in 20 g sugar and butter. Blend the rest of the ingredients in a thermo mixer. Mix 500 g of the cheese mix and 100 g sugar and pour in a form of 30x12cm, bake at 175ºC/350ºF for 17 minutes. For the thyme sablé make a dough of all the ingredients and bake in the oven at 180ºC/356ºF. For the marinade mix all ingredients and marinate the cubes of pineapple in it. For the parfait boil sugar and a bit of water at 117ºC/242ºF. Add to the egg yolks and beat to get a paté à bombe. Heat 200 g cream and infuse with thyme for about 10 minutes. Pour through a fine mesh sieve and add the pre-soaked gelatin. Mix this mass with the paté à bombe and carefully blend in the whipped cream using a spatula. For the sorbet heat part of the coulis with the glucose and the invert sugar and mix with the rest of the ingredients. Set aside to cool and spin. Arrange the mango tart between the sablé. Place a small piece of parfait on top and serve with the sorbet and marinated pineapple.

## Verbena soup with green apple and yogurt-pepper ice cream

*For the verbena soup:* 1 ltr water, 110 g sugar, 15 g lemon grass, 15 g verbena, 3 sheets of gelatin

*Jelly of green apple:* 600 g pulp of green apple, 115 g water, 3.8 g agar-agar, 2 sheets of gelatin.

*For honey jelly:* 75 g honey, 125 g water, 1.3 g agar-agar.

*For the lemon cream:* 15 g lemon zest, 150 g lemon juice, 2 eggs, 80 g butter, 100 g sugar.

*For the fennel:* 300 g sugar, 1 ltr water, fennel, Maria Brizard (Anise drink)

*For the foam of pineapple:* 1 ltr pineapple juice, 300 g Maria Brizard, 12 g lecithin.

*For the yogurt-pepper ice cream:* 225 g milk, 800 g yogurt, 5 g pink pepper, 40 g glycerin, 100 g pro-crema sosa (basis for ice cream), 40 g yogurt powder.

Heat all ingredients for the soup except the verbena and the gelatin. In a separate pan heat verbena and simmer for 4 minutes. Drain and add the pre-soaked gelatin. For the apple jelly, cook 1/3 of the pulp with water and agar-agar, add the rest of the ingredients and pour in a mould of 16 x 16cm to gel. For the honey jelly cook all ingredients together and pour over the apple jelly. For the lemon cream mix all ingredients except the butter and heat au bain-marie. Push through a fine mesh sieve and add the butter. For the fennel, boil water and sugar to make sugar water. Cook finely chopped fennel in this liquid and marinate each 100 g fennel with 30 g Maria Brizard. For the foam, mix lecithin with the other ingredients and create the foam with a blender. For the ice cream, heat milk and pepper, let simmer for ten minutes and mix with the rest of the ingredients. Cool, let rest for 4 hours and spin. Serve as shown in the photo.

## Carrot plum cake with coconut and orange sorbet

*For the orange sorbet:* 1 ltr orange juice, 25 g lemon juice,
30 g Mandarin Napoleon, 150 g invert sugar, 30 g glucose,
6 g sorbet stabilizer, zest of ½ orange.
*For the carrot plum cake:* 3 eggs, 15 g corn starch, 100 g orange
juice, 150 almond powder, 50 g white rum, 200 g coarsely
grated carrot, peel of 1 orange.
*For the carrot jelly:* 440 g fresh strained carrot juice, 6 g gellan,
1 sheet of gelatin.
*For the coconut mousse:* pulp of 1 coconut, 400 g slightly
whipped cream, 120 g sugar, 8 sheets of gelatin.
*For the candied carrot strips:* carrot, 1 ltr water, 400 g sugar.
*For the ginger-lime tapioca:* 650 g water, 80 g sugar, 20 g lemon-
grass, 15 g ginger, 50 g tapioca, fresh ginger juice, lime juice.

For the sorbet, heat part of the orange juice with the glucose, invert
sugar and stabilizer and mix with the rest of the requested ingredients.
Cool and spin. For the plum cake, separate the eggs; beat egg yolks with
half the sugar, add almond powder, cornstarch and orange peel and
finally add the rum and carrot. Beat egg whites with sugar and spoon
carefully through the mixture. Bake the cake at 175°C/350°F for
35 minutes in the oven. For the carrot jelly, heat the juice with the gellan
to 68°C/154°F, add the pre-soaked gelatin and pour over the plum cake.
For the coconut mousse, whip the cream until just fluffy. Dissolve the
gelatin in the coconut pulp and when it starts to droop, add the whipped
cream. For the candied carrot strips, thinly slice the carrots with a
vegetable peeler. Make sugar water with water and sugar and blanch the
carrot strips. For the tapioca boil water and sugar and simmer with the
ginger and lemon grass. Drain and cook the tapioca in this liquid.
Add 12 g ginger juice and 12 g lime juice for every 100 g cooked tapioca.
Before serving warm the tapioca in the microwave. Serve as shown in
the photo.

# Rigiblick
*Beatrice Zwicker-Eggler*

Just outside the centre of Zurich, Switzerland, is restaurant Rigiblick. The name is derived from the mountain Rigi that you can see from a distance only on very clear days. Beatrice Zwicker-Eggler has been the chef pâtissier of this star restaurant for four years. After her study in pâtisserie she continued in the restaurant kitchen, which she found more intensive and dynamic than the confectionary. Her desserts stand out in their techniques and structures. Beatrice feels that flavours should not be too heavy and should have a good balance.

www.rigiblick.ch

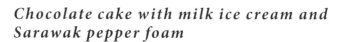

### Chocolate cake with milk ice cream and Sarawak pepper foam

*For four people:* 8 meringue sticks, 4 pepper florentines.
*For the cake:* 400 g butter, 500 g milk chocolate, 200 g egg yolk, 100 g sugar, 100 g cognac, 80 g sifted flour, 300 g egg white, 50 g sugar.
*For the milk ice cream:* 350 g milk, 140 g egg yolk, 50 g sugar, 150 g cream, 100 g feuilletine.
*For the pepper foam:* 500 g cream, 25 g sugar, ½ tsp ground Sarawak pepper, marrow of 1 vanilla bean, 1 sheet of gelatin, 125 g egg yolk, 50 g sugar.

For the cake melt the chocolate in the butter. Beat egg yolks and sugar until foamy, add the cognac and then the flour using a spatula. Beat egg whites and sugar until stiff and add to the mixture with the spatula. Pour the batter in a mould lined with parchment paper and bake at 180ºC/355ºF for 25 minutes. The cake will cave in, but that is normal. For the ice cream, heat milk, cream and sugar and pour on top of the egg yolks and prepare as an anglaise. Cool, strain and spin in the ice cream machine. Lastly add feuilletine and mix carefully. For the foam, heat sugar, pepper and the vanilla marrow. Whisk egg yolk with sugar to a smooth consistency and pour the hot mixture on top. Let cool and add the soaked gelatin. Pour the mixture in a siphon, let cool and insert two chargers. Cut the cake in squares, put a quenelle of ice cream on top and garnish with a pepper florentine. Pipe the foam in a glass and garnish with the meringue.

## Tropical smoothie

*For 4 people:* peppermint, chocolate curl.
*For the smoothie:* 500 g milk, 200 g yogurt, 200 g pulp of
mango and passion fruit, juice and peel of 1 lime, 40 g honey,
mineral water.
*For the banana:* 4 baby bananas, 40 g sugar, 30 g butter,
100 ml orange juice, 4 ml dark rum, 1 cm ginger, 1 vanilla bean,
1 star anise.
*For the chocolate sauce:* 100 ml milk, 100 ml cream, 200 g dark
chocolate, sugar.
*For the cardamom ice cream:* 250 g coconut milk, 200 ml cream,
½ Tbs ground cardamom, peel and juice of 1 lime, 120 g sugar,
100 g egg yolk.
*For the banana tuille:* 100 g bananas, 30 g sugar, 40 g melted
butter, 200 ml milk, 40 g cornstarch.

For the smoothie: mix the requested ingredients. For the banana,
caramelize the sugar and fry the bananas slightly in it, take out of
the pan. Add the spices to the pan, deglaze with the juice and flambé
with the rum. Put bananas back in the pan, caramelize and mix
the sauce with the butter.
Heat milk and cream, add chocolate and stir till smooth. Add sugar to
taste. For the ice cream, heat coconut milk, the cream, the cardamom, the
lime peel and juice. Beat egg yolk with sugar and prepare as an anglaise.
Strain, cool and spin. For the tuille: caramelize the sugar, add the butter
and cook the bananas till done. Purée the cooled bananas and add the
milk and starch. Spread the batter thinly on a silpat and bake in the oven
at 170ºC/340ºF. Serve the smoothie in a small glass with a small straw.
Garnish the bananas with a piece of peppermint and a banana tuille.

D09

# Who we are

A crazy bunch of hard working food lovers

As an English speaking person, the name Culibooks probably doesn't mean much to you. This is our very first edition to be published in English, but that doesn't mean we are new at it.

Culibooks is not a large publishing company, on the contrary. We are a small team of crazy workers, who are constantly traveling to every corner of Europe to report on the latest trends and techniques.

Norbert and Carine Koreman created the company in 1995. Today, every chef and pâtissier in France, Belgium and The Netherlands knows our glossy magazines and books. We are well-known for our magazine with the black cover, Culinaire Saisonnier, which is published in French and Dutch. The goal of this magazine is to reach top gastronomic professionals. The publication even has its own chefs' club, Les Amis Saisonnier, which counts most of the Michelin stars of Europe in its membership. When you visit a gastronomic enterprise in Europe you might see our black oval shield on the façade of the building.

In 2006 our new pink magazine appeared on the European market: Pâtisserie & Desserts. Although many professionals in the industry questioned the pink colour, it became a great success. Since then the pink colour has often been associated with pastries in Europe. In some kitchens pâtissiers have even started to wear pink chefs jackets.

Why the pink colour? Simply because it reminds us of sweet candies when we were children, and as children we also learned that pastry meant parties and party decorations were often pink.

Culibooks is based in Belgium, close to Antwerp. In 2007 we discovered a little old factory, situated in a beautiful natural environment, and rebuilt it. Not only do we have our offices there, but also a full restaurant and pâtisserie kitchen, supplied with every possible technical tool imaginable. There is also a library with old cookbooks and even an authentic café. Because of our microclimate there, we are able to grow figs, kiwis, grapes and oranges, something that is not common in cold Belgium.

Our editors are all skilled professionals, either chefs or pâtissiers. When they discover new material or techniques during their travels in Europe, it is immediately tested in our professional kitchen.

Through "Pastry in Europe" we would like to share with you the tremendous know-how and expertise we have achieved over the years. Every year we will publish this rich, pink book in English, so that pastry chefs around the world can be informed of all the pastry happenings in Europe. We will include the newest techniques combined with the oldest traditions and introduce you to Europe's most skilled pastry professionals.

## We would like to introduce our team:

The publisher and chief editor is **Norbert Koreman**. He studied food technology and economics, but later specialized in culinary photography. Norbert loves North America. Proof of that are his cars in the parking lot: an Avalanche and an SSR.
His partner is **Carine Van Steen**. She is responsible for the administration.
The co-editor is **Joost van Roosmalen**, who is the driving force of Pastry in Europe. Joost used to be a chef in star restaurants and also worked in the culinary field in America. He is not only an editor but also a chef in our test kitchen. To show the world that he can still cook, he participated in the Dutch National Championship for chefs and won the silver medal.

**Philippe Schroeven** is our French language editor. He is specialized in the classic kitchen and does all the translations from the French language. **Danny Jansen** is the editor who is fully specialized in pastry. He used to work as a pâtissier in famous restaurants.
**Jeroen van Oijen** is also an editor who has specialized in pastry, but is mostly busy discovering new techniques and developing new ideas. **Hans Heiloo** is also a pâtissier with a passion. He used to work as a chef-pâtissier in the renowned Amstel Hotel in Amsterdam. His love is classic techniques.
Our editor **Etienne Van Steenberghe** is fully specialized in wines and is known as author of many wine books. People say that he knows all the winemakers in Europe!!!
Three people work on the photography and one of them is editor **Norbert Koreman**. Next to him are the two best photographers of Belgium: **Peter Staes** and **Dirk Kerstens**. The designer of the pastry books and magazines is **Geert Dijkers**. His ideas are developed by desktop publisher **Anja Nelis**, who also deals with all the print companies. The thousands of subscriptions and our Internet boutique are in the hands of **Martine Lallement** and **Kristel Pintjens**. In charge of marketing are **Harry Huisman** and **Hilde Van Tuyne**.
We have expanded our team for Pastry in Europe with some very special people. **Elly Driessen** takes care of all the translations and **Don Genova** is the final editor of the English edition. Both live on Vancouver Island in Canada.

# One Way
## The ideal piping bag

**The older generation amongst us can still remember the cotton piping bags that were hung to dry in each bakery and kitchen. They were replaced by more sterile material but that also had some drawbacks. Now we have a piping bag on the market that combines the new and the old.**

In 1996, when Jan van der Straaten started One Way Plastics he was not aware of the difficulties he would encounter over the years. "Thank goodness," he said. "Had I known, I might never had started." To realize his dream of developing a disposable piping bag that feels like a cotton piping bag with no problems, he had to make mountains move. When we walked through his production hall, in Oosterhout, in the south of Holland, we realized that this could not have been an easy task. Four extruders make their own different base product and melt these products to get an endless tube of green film. But not just film, there are four separate layers. Because of these four layers, the film that later

Sealing strenght test          Puncture resistance test                                    Seal and perforation station

transforms into a piping bag has all the qualities that you could wish for. The inside layer is smooth and forms an excellent seal. The second layer gives great strength and the third layer gives the elasticity. Totally new is the outside layer, which gives the One Way piping bag a soft and pleasant feel, and a good grip, even with wet or greasy hands.

Back to the production process: As soon as the four-layer film is ready, it is treated further using equipment of extreme precision. The seam of the bag is heat sealed and then perforated. Next, rolls are created which are put in a wall dispenser. Because of the perforated line, one can just pull off a piping bag. The film is made under high temperature, making the piping bag totally sterile.

## Blue, red, green

There are several quality control systems at One Way. To measure the strength of the Bags, strong pushing and pulling is applied. The thickness of the material is constantly measured and certified by European rules and regulations in the category food approvals. We see that the bag comes in different colours. Jan van der Straaten explains that each colour has a different function. The blue or transparent bag Cool Blue has 3 layers and is meant for cold and airy fillings. The red piping bag Red Hot, also consists of 3 layers, and is for thick and hot fillings. But Jan's favorite is the green piping bag, the Comfort Green, which consists, as mentioned, of 4 layers and this one is patented. All bags are available in different sizes. We feel that Jan van der Straaten and his One Way business is a great example of good product innovation, totally geared to the ideal wishes of each pâtissier, baker and chef. The products of One Way are available worldwide. If you would like more information on the Comfort Green piping bag, or if you would like a free sample sent to your home, visit the website **www.onewaypipingbags.com**

95

*P09*

Terroir

Europe has a wealth of traditions. In almost every village or city you will find specialties that should have gone from the earth a long time ago. We want to pay tribute to these dinosaurs.

The French word "Terroir" cannot be easily translated. It is a concept that combines climate, ground, traditions, craftsmanship, techniques and the human sentiment. We most often see the word terroir used in wine regions, but it also applies to the area of pâtisserie.

We offer a number of reports about people and their products with what we consider to be a strong terroir. There's that one Belgian village where they make "mattentaarten" and the medieval city of 's Hertogenbosh where they make a special shortcake in accordance with old traditions. In the north of France we discovered candies that were produced by accident and are now famous, and in the south of France we met a village baker who makes his own nougat.

*Geraardsbergse Mattentaart*

# Traditional Flemish tart

We are in the city of the original Manneken Pis, where the famous Brussels statue of a boy 'having a leak' has been displayed 160 years longer than in Brussels. However, Geraardsbergen, in the Flemish Ardennes, is more famous for its Mattentaart. Each café, each restaurant and each bakery has a sign at the front of their business that says this delicacy is available there.

What exactly is a mattentaart? This pastry was already made here in the Middle Ages. Matten in Flemish or Matton in French means something like drained curdled milk. Whole milk is brought to a boil at the farm.

Then buttermilk is added to create the separation. The curds are then put through a sieve and put through cheesecloth. The drained and dried curds are called matten, which explains the name of the mattentaart. The dry matten are put through a grinder and mixed with egg yolks, sugar and beaten egg whites. A layer of puff pastry is put in the bottom of a round tart form that has a serrated edge. The matten filling is then poured into the form and another layer of puff pastry put on top. A thin layer of egg yolk is brushed on top and several cuts are made in the middle of the dough, with a pair of scissors, so the moisture can evaporate. The cuttings form a little rose that appears after baking.

The tart will be baked at 250oC/480oF for 25 minutes. It is quite simple. Similar tarts can be found in Flanders and also in Wallonia, where it has the shape of a half moon.

## Not really a Baker

The Geraardsberge mattentaart has received the European certificate BGA (which means it is geographically protected), similar to the French AOC, and a source of great pride to the people of the city. Now, if you ask anyone here where you can find the most authentic mattentaart, people will undoubtedly point you in the direction of Olav Geerts. We find him in his store behind the counter where many mattentaarts are displayed in every size, as well as several other regional products. Olav is the 6th generation of a baker family: "The great grandfather of my grandfather started baking the mattentaart in 1780. The recipe passed on from father to son, I still have the original recipe. However, we don't bake them here, we just sell them". So the baker actually doesn't bake? "I am extremely busy in the community at the social-cultural level, and belong to the society of "Manneken Pis" and the Geraardsberge Mattentaart.
So everyone in this city tells tourists to come to me; it is a very authentic picturesque shop. But I get my mattentaarts from only one baker and that is Geert Vercleijen."
Olav Geerts started his business in 1980. At that time the mattentaart was not as well known as it is today. It has become very popular over the last 15 years, as the founding of the society in 1978 and the European recognition have helped build the fame. "Nobody who visits this city will leave without a mattentaart," says Olav. "Every resident in this city will always have a mattentaart at their home, just in case they get visitors or they take it to people if they go and visit. It is not a very sweet tart and can be eaten for breakfast or just as a snack. There are rumours that Rabobank cyclists eat these little tarts to gain extra energy before they go on a bicycling tour." We have one more question for Olav: Why is this tart so special only in Geraardsbergen? "The geographic protection of the BGA demands that the milk used to make the mattentaart can only come from Geraardsbergen and environs or the municipality of Lierde. The farmers have to make their own matten at the farm. The valley here has a specific climate that gives the milk its own taste. The bacteria in the curdled milk are distinctive to this region. Therefore, the tarts can only be baked in this area."

## The Trade

We leave Olav and quickly go to Geert Vercleijen, a man who still bakes his tarts the authentic way. Many bakers think they can enhance the tarts by adding almond essence or to spread a mixture of confiture or applesauce on the bottom of the tart. Geert does not believe in that. "I still bake only the traditional way. We have a team of six bakers and do everything by hand." We see a bakery shop full of metal forms or molds for small, medium and large tarts. The process is exactly as we have described earlier, but now we're seeing it all happen manually on a larger

scale. Two long tables are full of specific little forms. These are greased first and then lined with puff pastry. The bakers flatten small balls of dough tightly in the little molds. Another baker quickly follows by pouring the filling into the molds, using a piping bag. Another layer of puff pastry is firmly pressed on top. Every little tart is created by hand. It is finished with some brushed egg yolk, cuttings are made in the middle of the dough with scissors, and then the tarts are baked. Thousands of mattentaarts leave Geert's bakery. Seeing all of the action over the course of one hour made our jaws drop in amazement. It makes us feel good that these tarts cannot be imitated because of their official recognition and protection law. There are people who are trying to create the same thing, but the use of frangipane, potatoes, or other products used for the filling will be immediately penalized. You can never bake a "protected" Geraardseberge mattentaart yourself, unless you live in Geraardsbergen! You can prepare something similar, but then you can only call it mattentaart, never a Geraardseberge mattentaart! Thank you Geert, we have respect for your craft!

www.mattentaarten-delekkerbek.be

## Mattentaart

*Ingredients:* 7 litres whole milk, 2 litres farmer's buttermilk, 8 eggs, separated, 600 g white sugar, puff pastry, 1 extra egg yolk.

Boil the milk and add the buttermilk. The milk will now start to separate. Pour this through a sieve. Then put the solids in cheesecloth, drain completely and let dry. Mix 1 kilogram of the dry mixture with 550 grams of sugar and 8 egg yolks. Beat the egg whites with the rest of the sugar and carefully blend it all together with the use of a spatula. Put the greased little forms close together on a table and put one very thin layer of puff pastry over all of them. Then push the dough into the individual forms. Pour the filling into the forms and top with another very thin layer of puff pastry. Then remove the pastry from between each form and squeeze the two layers of dough tightly around the edge. Brush a thin layer of egg yolk over the dough and cut the middle with scissors, so that the moisture can evaporate. There seem to be different opinions on the baking time. We prefer to listen to Geert Vercleijen, who bakes his tarts at 250°C/480°F for 25 minutes. Then let them steam a little before taking them out of the tart form.

Dutch Breakfast Cake

# Bossche Koek

's Hertogenbosch might be one of the most French Burgundian-Dutch cities in the world. The very old city is where you will find the traditional koek of this story.

When we meet Gieljan and Sylvana De Backer, we immediately dive into Dutch history while enjoying the Bossche koek with a cup of coffee. On the outside this koek reminds you of other similar Dutch breakfast cakes, called peperkoek or ontbijtkoek, but when we taste this one, we realize that this is a totally different cake. This one is more refined in aroma and taste. The Bossche Koek is a traditional concept, because the recipe, with its different mix of spices, has been unchanged for centuries. It is believed that the famous 15th and 16th century painter, Jeroen Bosch, was familiar with this koek. Just like a French family hotel, where you will find a chair they tell you was once occupied by Napoleon, it is the same with cakes, tarts and sweets: every family has its own recipe with their own spices and flavors; a family secret, passed on from father to son, as with the case of the De Backer family. The making of their family koek started in 1865. Adrianus de Backer, a member of the Bossche baker family, committed the recipe to print in 1915 and gave it to his sons Jan and Egi. Jan continued the family koek tradition. The Bossche koek from Gieljan's father Jan was famous in Holland and beyond. The cake gained its fame as Jan De Backer sold them in wicker baskets to tourists who were visiting the St. Jans' Cathedral. After years of hard work, Jan passed away in 1988, just a few weeks after he retired. He must have taken the recipe to his grave, as the written recipe had been lost for years. It seemed that the family recipe had been lost forever, until a small miracle twenty-three years later. In 2001, while they were building a café on the site of Jan's former home and bakery, Gieljan's son Jules saw something sticking out of a canvas wall, which turned out to be the lost recipe! Partially eaten by mice, but still readable, the Bossche koek of Jan de Backer was reborn...

## Figuring out the Recipes

Old recipes are totally different than the ones we use today. For successor Gieljan, who has no background in baking, recipes were like secret codes. He and his wife Sylvana called on several old bakers and experts to get help. Old fashioned ingredients like alum and ammonia were replaced with products of today. Happy with the results, the proud couple decided to give the koek back to the city with great success. The bakers, who had helped them deciphering the recipes, got permission to bake the koek themselves, but only receive the dough after it has been made by the De Beckers. While we are visiting, the couple behaves nervously and is afraid somebody is spying on them. They are afraid that the production will lose its special nature if someone other than them makes the dough and passes it on to another baker. We have to smile a bit with all this secrecy, because we know pretty well how this koek is produced. We are also familiar with the production of peperkoek. Still, the secrecy has its charm, so we play the game.

For this, we visit Baker Daniël van Schijndel, who receives his dough in small wooden containers. The only thing he has to do is sprinkle sugar candy over it and bake it. He knows nothing about the recipe, but tells us how the process of making the koek works. A peperkoek is created with a starter dough mixed with rye flour, sugars, water, salt and old Bossche koek. The old koek provides the extra taste and binding. The sugars are cooked to make a syrup at 98oR, which together with the other ingredients forms the dough. This dough has to rest for at least 3 days. It is sometimes called rest dough. This dough looks very grey and dull and it is hard to imagine that at some point it will become a delicious treat. After that, one starts with the second part of the dough, which is sometimes called the breakthrough of the dough. The second part consists of extremely secret spices and flavours, sugar coated fruits, honey and rice. The spice mix may vary, but the most commonly used spices are cinnamon, nutmeg, ginger, cardamom, cloves, white pepper, coriander seeds and mace. The dough is put in small thin wooden containers lined with parchment paper. Just as in the early days, the small containers are baked in a wooden mold. The wooden mold is necessary to avoid burnt crusts on the sides. The koek is baked at 180oC/350oF for 80 minutes. A good koek should not be eaten for a few weeks, maybe even a few months to get the maximum flavour of the spices. This is one of the reasons that sailors ate peperkoek as they could be safely stored for a long voyage at sea. Sylvana and Gieljan personally check Daniël van Schijndel's koek. They break it in half with culinary flair and check the structure, scent and taste. The koek is definitely not dry and sticks to your fingers. This is because of the sugarcoated orange and lemon peel, the honey and the caramelized candied sugar. Gieljan secretly tells us that there are 30 ingredients in the koek, including 8 spices. The Bossche koek is a very important item in Daniël's shop; he sells about 80 per week, small and large. At this point we would like to visit the other bakery, where the dough is made, but are told that it is strictly prohibited. Gieljan promises us that he will take pictures and send them to us. We assume that the Pentagon has less security. You can find a recipe for making a bomb on the Internet, but not for making a Bossche koek...

However, it is possible to find bakers in 's Hertogenbosch who are making their own Bossche koek. Gieljan shrugs his shoulders, saying all those recipes have changed many times over the years. He is the only one who can take credit for authentic formula of the past.

### Yes, still a recipe...

The scientific part of the Bossche koek is a big secret; but we don't want to disappoint you, so here is a recipe. When you start working with this, you might come close to making the authentic article.

*For the starter dough:* 540 g rye flour, 200 g glucose, 120 g fructose, 160 g water, 50 g old koek, 100 g candied sugar.
*For the second part:* 25 g honey, 90 g baking powder, 50 g spice mix of your own choice, 50 g sugar coated fruits.

Starter dough: cook water and sugar and the old koek at 96ºR and mix with the flour and later with the candied sugar. Let dough rest for at least 3 to 7 days. For the second part, mix the dough with the honey, the spices and the sugarcoated fruits, pour into a mould and bake at 180ºC/350ºF for 80 minutes.

# Bêtises de Cambrai

Nowadays, it seems that our industry can only talk about revolutionary new pastry techniques using agar-agar, soy-lecithin, cryo-technique and spherification. There are indeed millions of ways to create sweet things; fortunately there are still time-honored traditions. We discovered this in northern France, in the little village of Cambrai, with a recipe that has been unchanged since 1859.

The word bêtise simply means stupidity, and stupidity played a key role in the history of a famous candy. When we started to do research on this candy we came upon a "stupid" bakery student: Emile Afchain. Over two centuries ago this character worked at the pastry shop of his parents. When he made a crucial mistake while he was preparing his candies, his mother yelled: "Your candies have gone to pot. You are not capable of doing anything. Again a bêtise!" But miraculously this bad candy became a huge success! The recipe was written down and a new product created, which was the result of stupidity. The baking industry discovered you could make a lot of money with the bêtise and now everyone claims that they are making the original bêtise.

## From one story to the next

A few kilometers outside the center of Cambrai, in the little village of Fontaine-Notre Dame, we find the shop of Despinoy, a small artisan confiserie. François Campion, the maître confiseur and owner, gives us

a warm welcome. We asked to learn more about the history of the bêtise. Campion: "There are many stories going around, but I really don't know the true story. It is believed, that in the early days, the men who were visiting the annual traditional market, which took place for several days, took a box of candies home, to hide their stupidity. Another story is much more related to my shop. In 1850, there was a student working for Jules Despinoy, and this student burnt the sugar. To disguise this, he started to pull on the sugar, in the hope of getting it white again."
We explained that we had read this story in full on the Internet in which a certain Afchain played the key character. François looked at us in shock: "The liars! The story of Jules Despinoy has existed much longer."
It turns out there has always been a lot of rivalry between the families of Afchain and Despinoy, even in the courts. In 1889 a judge ruled Afchain was deemed to be the inventor of the bêtise, while Despinoy was chosen to be the maker. At that time, this hilarious story was picked up by the French Press and published in all the newspapers, which made this

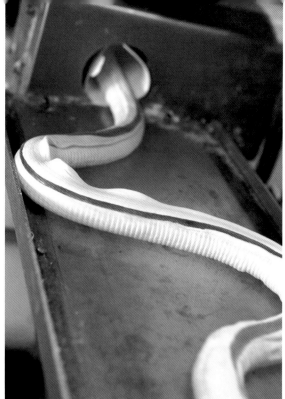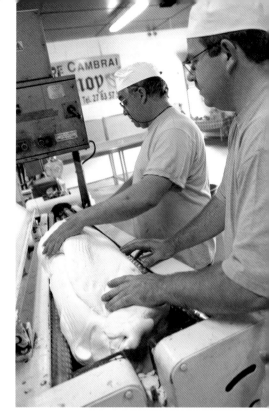

candy very famous. The result? Many cities started to make their own bêtises, even in Belgium. In the Belgian city of Tournay (Doornik) this candy is called sotisse, which means exactly the same as stupidity.

## Pure coincidence

The candy adventure for Francois Campion started because his father, who was a brewer, fell in love with Mrs. Despinoy, who wanted to sell her business. The father accepted her offer but paid very little attention to the confiserie. Francois, the son, had no intention to become a brewer, but the candy business did attract him. This was in 1990. The father was very lucky to get the help of a 92 year old man, the last maître-confiseur of Despinoy. "Life was tough in the beginning", says Francois. "In those days my wife and I worked with one large copper pot and a wooden mill, which we had to turn by hand. The first year we produced 10 tonnes of bêtises, last year 130 tonnes". But in spite of that hardship, he still cherishes the beginning. "The sugar was much better when we worked

with the copper pot. Because of the new laws on hygiene I was forced to use different material." But the basic recipe never changed, with mint as the most important base. Francois uses a combination of saccarose and glucose. In the early days he used corn sugar, but because of all the controversy over genetically modified corn and the difficulty in obtaining non-GM corn, he doesn't trust use corn sugar anymore. The sugar mixture is heated to 140C/285oF and then spread on a cool slab. He used to use marble, but that is also prohibited now. Part of the sugar is colored with caramel; the rest is treated in a pulling machine for 5 minutes. This gives the sugar 25 to 30 per cent more volume. Both sugar concoctions are then combined and pulled through the laminoir (mill). The caramelized sugar gives the candy a yellow stripe. The candies are now ready to be cut and wrapped, and are processed at 500 pieces per minute. Knowing the history of competition and rivalry of this candy, we wanted to know what the secret is of making the best bêtise. François: "Everything has to be natural. For example, we do not use coloring. I also

feel that the material we use should come from local sources as much as possible, because that's the way it happened in the past, except for the mint alcohol, which comes from Grasse. They have the best quality. I use two different kinds of alcohol, one with Brazilian mint, and the other with Chinese mint. That combination refines the candies. That is my secret!"

## Today and tomorrow

Sadly, there used to be 10 producers in Cambrai, but only Despinoy and Afchain are left. Surviving the confiserie-sector means some sacrifices to the artisan nature of the candy-makers. Initially Francois Despinoy did not want anything to do with supermarkets. But because of some large brand names in this sector, he slowly started to trust them. "I am not embarrassed that my candy is now available in the supermarket as well. More and more people are interested in gummy candies; they have almost forgotten that we have beautiful products in France." François's bêtises are now sold under six different labels, including the very well known Reflets de France in France. "They asked me to change the recipe for them, but there is no way. I would rather quit!" However, he is sensitive to the world that asks for diversity. Therefore, he makes bêtises of apple, raspberry, violet, praline/orange and chocolate/orange. To him they are not real bêtises, but he has to survive as a businessman as well as an artisan.

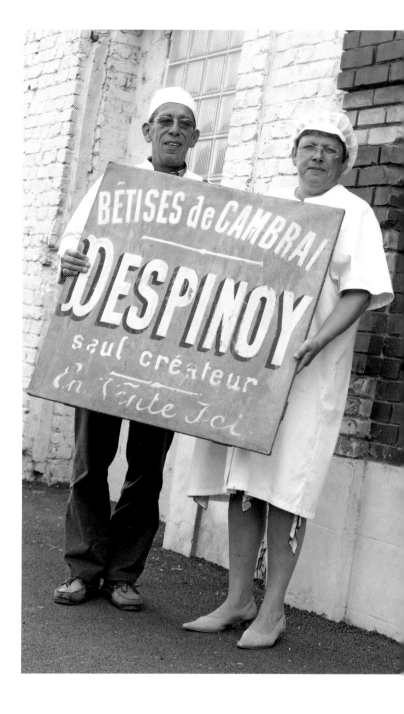

*Black Nougat*

# Traditions keep

The Lozère is the poorest and sparsest population region of France. The nature is spectacular, but there is not much else to find. It is in regions such as this that traditions can stay alive for many centuries, also in pâtisserie.

# going

In the picturesque little village of Florac, at the ravines of the Gorges du Tarn, you will find Stéphane Marquis, the pâtissier of the village. He can be proud of his business experience, as he worked with Monsieur Billet, a Meilleur Ouvrier de France, (best craftsman of France). Why did he start his own business ten years ago? "Being independent gives you the privilege to make your own decisions." Stéphane stays in the workshop and his wife Nadine is in the store and sells a large assortment of regional products. Our pâtissier specializes in working with chestnuts in a large variety of ways, which we will mention in more detail in another edition. We want to tell you about the way he listens to the sound of almonds, the reason we are giving you his recipe of black nougat.

The village of Florac

P09

Listening to the sounds of the singing...

## Black Nougat

*Ingredients:* 800 g almonds with skin, 800 g natural honey,
2 sheets of edible sweet paper.

Grease a baking frame of 2cm high, 50 cm long and 10 cm wide. Put this frame on a wooden board covered with parchment paper and put one sheet of edible paper in the form. Clean a copper pan with wine vinegar and fine salt (this should always be done before making a caramel) and cook the honey in it. Make sure your pan is large enough as the honey will start to bubble. Keep the honey running so it will not crystallize.

The next moment is crucial for a good result, but is hard to describe. Stéphane Marquis does it just by looking at it. Now and then he takes a spoon, puts a drop on the stove and lets it cool. This should turn out dark and hard. At that time, the almonds are added. The pan is still on the stove and the mixture is constantly stirred with a wooden spatula. Now, our pâtissier listens carefully so he can hear the almonds sing! The sounds should be like pssizz, pssizz. If you hear a cracking sound, you have gone too far. When the singing is perfect, the mixture is then poured in a form, covered with another sheet of edible paper and pressed tightly on top. This is done with another wooden board, so the form is locked between two wooden boards. This is not just practical because

of the high temperature, but also because wood prevents fast cooling. The nougat is released when it has cooled down. Then the excess of edible paper is cut off, and the nougat cut into slices of 15 mm wide. But don't wait too long or the cutting will be very difficult. The nougat is well sealed so no moisture can get in. The result is beautiful to look at; the caramel is almost black, while the almonds stay white. Doesn't this nougat stick to your teeth? No, because honey is used. It would be totally different with sugar. The black nougat is part of thirteen desserts, which is traditionally eaten on Christmas Eve. Every time the clock strikes at midnight, the black nougat goes into someone's mouth…

*D09*

# Licorice
## The calvinistic candy

**You must know that the Dutch, more than any other people in Europe, are addicted to licorice. With 30 million kilos consumed every year, the Netherlands is number one, so we felt it necessary to look deeper into this black magic...**

In short, licorice is an infusion of the root juice of the licorice plant. The extract obtained is dried which is called blokdrop. This forms the base for further preparations. The blokdrop is infused again and after many additions put into little forms. The word drop came out of nowhere and is probably as Dutch as the candy itself. In Germany it is called lakritzen, in England it is called liquorice and in France they name it réglisse. However these words refer more to the licorice plant than to the actual drop.

## The most important ingredients

The root of the licorice plant is one of its most important parts. The shrub, lycyrrhiza uralensis, can be found in the Mediterranean area, China, Syria and Iran. The plant grows about 1.5 meters tall and thrives in moist areas along riverbanks. Sometimes the roots are at least 3 meters in the ground. It takes four years for a plant to mature and is harvested in October. At that time part of the roots are left untouched so they can be harvested the year after. When the roots are pulled up, they are untangled and dried in the sunshine to avoid mould. The dried roots will keep for months. The licorice root contains the sweetener glycyr-rhizine, which is 30 to 40 times sweeter than crystal sugar. The aroma is like fennel and anise. The salt flavour of drop often comes from salmiak with the chemical name ammoniumchloride. The salt is formed by the combination of acidic salt and ammoniak, in which case both components become harmless. The word salmiak originates from the French word salé ammoniaque, which means ammonium salt. Although we encourage being creative, we do not advise making salmiak yourself. You can get it in candy stores. Besides sugar, sometimes up to 60%, there are also other aromatic and flavours in drop. These can be natural, like bay leaf, anise, eucalyptus, honey and menthol. However it is often the chemical stuff which is doing the work. Drop is not black when it is produced but transparent and light brown. The candy is coloured with dark caramel or carbon.

Gum Arabic was once used for binding, but because of the high demand the price has increased. It is a resin material from the bark of an acacia tree that grows in Sudan and Senegal. Now potato starch or cornstarch is used instead.

## The Process

As mentioned before licorice root is a key element in the making of drop. After the roots have been dug up, cleaned and dried, it is all ground to a pulp. The pulp is reduced to a mush that is first filtered and then poured into tins. When this has hardened we call it blokdrop and is the base for all kinds of licorice. Lots of blokdrop comes from Italy wrapped in bay leaves that give it a nice extra flavour. Most of the blokdrop is exported to America, for large-scale use by the tobacco industry to give cigarettes their flavour. Part of it goes also to the pharmaceutical industry where it is efficiently used in cough syrup.

In the drop factory the blokdrop is dissolved in water with glucose, molasses and colouring agents. Then other ingredients like sugar, starch and other flavours are added. Honey-drop contains honey (or depending on the factory just a honey aroma) and the salty variety has more salmiak. Later the mixture is brought to taste and boiled at 135ºC/275ºF. From there the drop liquid goes to the casting factory where the drop candies are formed. Flexi pans are not used; most producers use moulds made of plaster and dusted with starch. After the drop has been poured, it has to dry two days in special rooms. The temperature in these rooms starts around 65ºC/150ºF and goes down to 20ºC/68ºF. After the drying process the drop candies are blown out of the moulds and the starch can be re-used. The drop candies are finished in a small kitchen mill, made of cement and coated with a glaze of beeswax and oil. Besides the regular drop candies there is also a variety of pressed drop, like drop laces and drop sticks.

## Licorice in the Kitchen

Working with licorice in a restaurant kitchen is uncommon, although the Dutch chef Pierre Wind became known for his chicken drumsticks with drop sauce! Sometimes we see crème brulee made of licorice on a dessert menu. It is probably the black colour that turns people off, because the taste of licorice root, anise and even salmiak are well liked. We do have a basic recipe for you, although it will most likely taste different than the commercial versions.

*Ingredients:* 8 sticks of licorice root, 500 ml water, 6 tsp syrup, 1 tsp salmiak, 2 gelatin leaves, 6 tsp cornstarch.

Cut the licorice root in small pieces and bring to a boil with the water. Let simmer for 5 minutes and pour through a sieve in a different pot, reduce the liquid to 100 ml, and then add the salmiak and syrup. Make a paste with the cornstarch and add to the simmering liquid. Stir well so the mixture will be smooth with no lumps. Add the pre-soaked gelatin. Then pour on greased foil and let harden for several days.

## Different kinds of licorice

An encyclopedia would not be big enough to describe all the kinds of licorice. The average producer seems tempted to create a new drop candy every day. However, some of the classics are worth mentioning:

**Honey drop** contains honey and is good for the throat.
**Mint drop** has a soft and sweet taste. Often this is combined with eucalyptus and menthol.
**Double salt drop** is an attack on your taste buds
**Katjes** (cats) drop has a typical ginger taste.
**Pepper balls** are a typical variety of Scandinavia; a hard little ball that is spiced with pepper.
**Griotten** are covered in sugar.
**Laurier** (bay leaf) drop, is a great combination of the taste of licorice and bay leaf.

## Drawing little foams

In the modern gastronomic kitchen we often see foam sauces presented on a dinner plate. That is nothing compared to the foam making that was done in the early days in the south of the Netherlands. It is a quite simple procedure. Pieces of very hard laurier drop were put in a bottle of water. That bottle had to be placed in a dark location for at least one day and night. To create a lot of foam you had to shake the bottle really hard. Sucking from that bottle was a real pleasure for children.

Please note that this only works with laurier drop. Maybe we can find a pâtissier who can create a modern creation of this variety!

We finally found the classic traditional German pâtisserie we were looking for. West of Berlin, close to Tiergarten Park, is a business with a rich history: Bäckerei (bakery) Buchwald at the Bartningallee. The bakery features a showcase full of large cakes that are sold by the slice. The establishment goes back to 1852 and was built by Onkel Gustav the First. The business became famous for their Baumkuchen and it was such a success that they even delivered to the royal family. According to the people from Berlin, Buchwald has become the place where the best Baumkuchen is made.

# Baumkuchen

At the far end of the store we found the bakery, where it looks and feels like time has come to a standstill. We were surprised that they still use a scale with weights and decagrams. People work very hard. The Konditoreimeister (master pâtissier) is the king of the baumkuchen and says: "The cakes consist of many layers that are baked piece by piece on top of each other." It reminds us of very thin-layered cakes, called spekkoek in Dutch, but without the spices. He was quite willing to give us his recipes.

### Baumkuchen

*Ingredients:* 250 g almond powder, 3 kg sugar, 3 kg flour, 3 kg butter (melted), 80 g baking powder, 800 g marzipan, 3 ltr eggs, 1½ ltr egg yolks, the seeds scraped from 10 vanilla beans, 5 Tbs cinnamon powder, 50 g lemon zest.

Melt the butter with a bit of water. Mix the sugar with the marzipan, the vanilla seeds, the cinnamon and the lemon juice. Beat eggs and egg yolks fluffy with the sugar, slowly add the melted butter and carefully add the flour and baking powder.

The Buchwald bakery makes 20 litres of this batter each day. The most interesting part is actually the preparation. In the corner stands a big oven with six large iron spits (rotisserie spikes) covered with aluminum foil. "It is almost like a large kebab grill," says the chef. "The Baumkuchen is a cake that gets cooked in an open fire." The process starts and the machine gets into action. Each spit is rolled through the batter and then baked by the warmth in the back of the oven. Werner points to a few small rings that are attached to the batter container. "That is my computer, because these rings tell me how many times the spits have gone through the batter. Every time it turns another ring is formed." Delicately the chef checks if there are no extra residues on the batter and with his finger he checks if the dough is done. Although we are several metres away from the oven, we see the sweat pouring off the chef's back. Werner is used to this heat and just smiles. After five turns through the batter we see a comb appear. This gives the cakes their special cachet. With an extra finesse the comb is pushed against the fresh batter, but not against the batter that is baked. "It is a carefully executed process, because we don't want to damage the baked layers as that would cause lumps in the batter."

Werner can control the colour by the speed of the rotisserie in the oven, but the temperature stays constant. The slower the rotation, the browner the cake. Slowly we start to recognize the cake as we know it and after nine layers it is done. Werner gives it some extra turns to deepen the colour. It takes a full day before the cakes have cooled off and can be finished. The spits are then removed from the cakes and what is left looks like a long accordion of Baumkuchen. The cakes are garnished with apricot jelly with fondant or chocolate and then cut in different sizes and wrapped. It is not a cheap cake: they cost about 35 euros per kilogram.

There are two different ways to make Baumkuchen. Werner only uses the Cotbusse method. The other method comes from the village Salzwedel. The difference is that they use a different kind of marzipan and no almond shavings in the batter. We feel a bit sick after eating the rich Baumkuchen and are ready to move on.

Although in previous city reportages we used mostly public transportation, on this trip we used the GPS in the car as our guide. The truth must be said: Berlin is a great city to drive in. Hardly any traffic jams and lots of free parking!

# The Rose and the Pig

Working with marzipan is a festive occasion. At Easter we make bunnies and who has never eaten marzipan piggies at Christmas? And then there are the wedding cakes, decorated with bright red roses. Working with marzipan is a craft that is often overlooked.

We land on the Dutch polder of Flevoland, where we meet Johan Gort, a craftsman in making marzipan. What started as a hobby has grown into a small business with great results. However, he assures us that he wants to continue to be a pastry maker, as he doesn't consider himself a businessman. But the only thing Johan and his staff do is work with marzipan. Little wedding cakes, animals, roses, carnations and lots of other flowers are created in a professional and creative way. They work with more than 250 kilograms of marzipan a week. The working day is almost over when we enter his workspace, but we can still feel the warm ambiance and hospitality. Johan only works with women, ten to be exact. "Besides the fact that these ladies create a comfortable atmosphere, they are more detail oriented and faster than men. I am proud of my harem!" That they seem to have a very congenial relationship is proof that teamwork is important to him. While they are cleaning up, Johan ponders that it is a shame that so many pastry makers do not know the basic technique of working with marzipan. According to him, it is not all that difficult, as long as you know the basics.

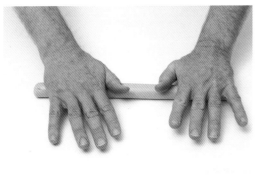

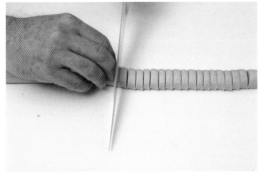

## The Rose

The ladies have gone home and per our request, Johan starts to demonstrate some of the basic techniques. You don't see many tools on the working bench, but a set of molding tools is essential. He shows that tools do not have to be expensive as he uses a piece of a PVC pipe to use as a rolling pin. The most important tool is your hands! First, a drop of sunflower oil is spread on the table to avoid stickiness. "You can use icing sugar, but I use that more for the bottom of flat pieces, as icing sugar shows". We start with a little rose. He creates a seamless little ball and rolls that in a form of a pill, which is cut in slices. He uses a little scraper to quickly create flower petals. The roses can consist of six, eight, or even twelve little petals. He finishes by creating little green leaves. Only one pin is used to finish the work. In Johan's shop, thousands of identical roses are created daily. Identical? Each of the ladies can recognize their own roses out of the thousands!

P09

## The Pig

Our next item is a little pig. According to Johan, the most important part is the making of oval shapes and round balls, which is important for all bodies. The little figurines all have a funny face and according to our teacher, it should be that way. "It is a caricature and we have to keep it that way, with figurines as well as flowers." Starting with the basic little body, the pink piggy is created with a little head, cheeks, ears, the snout, the bum and the little curly tail. The eyes are made last. He gives us a tip: a figurine should always look at a certain direction, no matter which way. A marzipan animal that looks straight ahead is a dead object and has no sparkle. The pupils of the eyes are black, made with norit (activated carbon). The rest of his colour selection is made of colored powders that prevent the forming of mold. Good quality of the materials is of utmost importance. Johan teaches us that it starts with the marzipan. If the marzipan is too stiff, the molding will be very difficult. Therefore, the best working temperature is 21°C/70°F. The kind of marzipan is also very important and you do not want to skimp on quality. Johan chooses the famous marzipan from Lübeck 1:3. This ratio is finer than the coarser one of 1:2, both made of 100% Spanish almonds. In the meantime Johan has prepared another figurine he wants to show us, revealing the importance of details. The body is usually the same but the head is quite different. If a head has long ears, it is a rabbit or pony, but if they look like little balls or pointed tips, it is a hippopotamus or a horse. We ask Johan how we can best preserve marzipan. He says the freezer is the best solution, as long as the marzipan is vacuum packed, as moisture is the worst enemy of marzipan. Does Johan not meet people who think they know it all or better? He laughs. "Of course there are always people who claim they can make better roses and I will admit that, but I always tell them they can call me in a case of emergency, as I like to help them. Most of the time, this means that I have gained another client for life!"

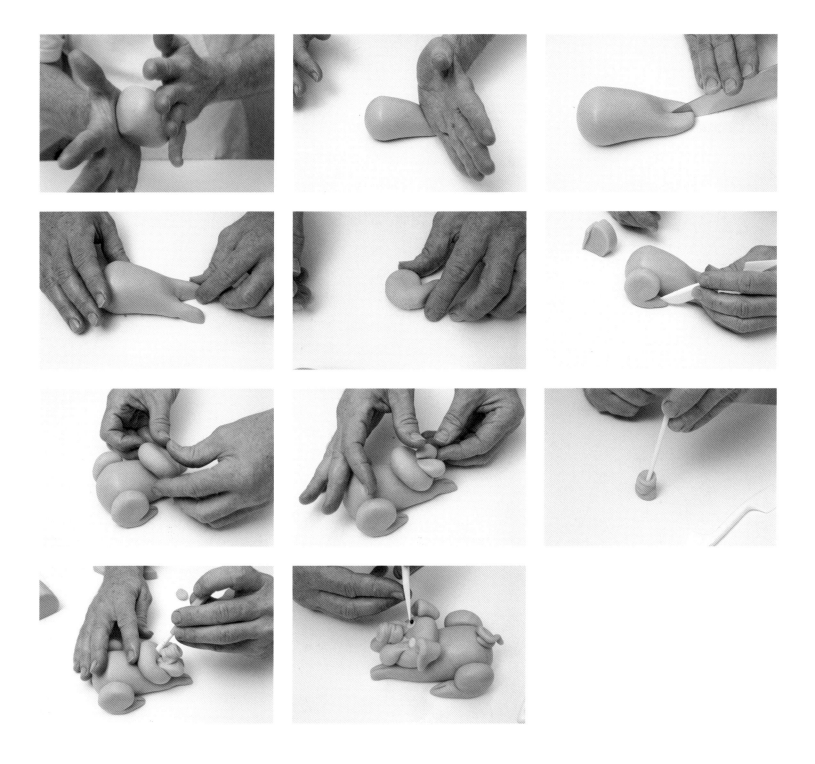

# Carme Ruscalleda

Carme Ruscalleda, at age 56, has been
recognized worldwide for her re-inter-
pretation of the Catalonian kitchen.
Her work was awarded with three
Michelin stars for restaurant Sant Pau
(San Pol de Mar, Catalonia, Spain)
and with two stars for Sant Pau in
Tokyo. Ruscalleda was brought up
with traditional recipes and uses
her creativity to incorporate these in
her cooking.

## New Crema Catalana

*1 ltr milk, peel of 1/2 a lemon, ½ stick cinnamon, 140 g sugar, 50 g wheat flour, 10 egg yolks.*

Bring milk, lemon peel, and cinnamon stick to a boil. Take pan off the heat, cover and let rest for 30 minutes. Filter the milk and divide in two equal portions. Mix one of the portions with the wheat flour and the sugar, heat this while mixing it and cook for 1 minute. Take pan off the burner and add the other portion of milk. Carefully add the egg yolks and keep cooking it but make sure it doesn't get hotter than 80°C/175°F. Divide over 8 bowls. Keep stirring so the texture doesn't change. Put in the fridge. For people who like a small layer of burnt sugar, heat a small kitchen iron on the fire. Sprinkle sugar over the bowls and burn top layer with the hot iron.

## Chocolate torró with pine nuts, almonds and pistachios

*For the white chocolate paste: 150 g white chocolate, 200 g pine nuts.*
*For the dark chocolate paste: 125 g dark chocolate (70% cocoa), 175 g roasted pine nuts.*
*For the crunchy nuts: 100 g peeled and roasted pistachios, 100 g roasted and slivered almonds.*

Melt white chocolate with pine nuts in a thermomixer at 40°C/104°F to make a soft creamy sauce. Pour in a cake form the size of a large rectangular chocolate tablet and spread a layer on the bottom. Divide the pistachio nuts on top of the white chocolate and press softly on to the mix. Heat the dark chocolate and the roasted pine nuts in the thermo mixer at 40°C/104°F. If you don't have a thermomixer melt au bain marie, but also not hotter than 40°C/104°F. Pour the chocolate over the layer of pistachio nuts. Divide the broken almond pieces over everything and press softly on to the dark chocolate layer. Put all of it in a cool, dark spot uncovered for 24 hours so the chocolate can harden. The torró stays good for three weeks if it is wrapped in aluminum foil and stored in a dry and cool spot.

# Régis Marcon

In the little village of Saint-Bonnet-le-Froid, home of the three-star restaurant Le Clos des Cimes, you will always encounter the seasons. Between Ardèche and the Auvergne, at an elevation of 1100 metres, you will find spring and summer blooms, the warm colours of fall, and the bright white of winter. It is in the coldest season that Régis Marcon, together with chef-pâtissier Christophe Gasper, takes the time to develop new creations. Régis is fortunate to have a pâtisserie laboratory and his very own bakery. Many chefs started pâtisserie at an older age, but not Régis. He started his career with chocolate and sugar. He will never forget his cooking with sugars.

**www.regismarcon.fr**

## Exquisite chocolate with granité of chicory

*For the chocolate puff pastry:* 100 g dark chocolate 62%, 120 g baked puff pastry, 50 g cocoa butter.
*For the chocolate génoise:* 16 eggs, 500 g sugar, cocoa powder, 250 g flour, 250 g cornstarch.
*For the waffle dough:* 30 g butter, 100 g brown sugar, 50 g egg white, 30 g flour.
*For the whipped ganache:* 450 g cream, 50 g glucose, 50 g trimoline, 357 g dark chocolate 62%, 95 g cream.
*For the chocolate sauce:* 100 g sugar, 60 g cocoa powder, dash of salt, 12 ml water,
*50 ml orange juice.*
*For the chocolate sorbet:* 1200 g water, 300 g glucose, 170 g cocoa powder, 200 g dark chocolate 62%, 8 g stabilizer, 8 g monosterat.
*For the granité of chicory:* 1 liter coffee, 200 g sugar, 5 g chicory.

For the chocolate puff pastry, melt the chocolate and the cocoa butter, add the puff pastry and spread on a slab to make pieces of 8 x 3 cm. For the waffle dough, melt the butter and the sugar, carefully fold in the egg whites and flour and bake the waffles in the oven at 170ºC/338ºF. For the génoise, beat eggs and sugar until white. Carefully blend in the flour, cocoa powder and cornstarch. Bake in the oven at 180ºC/355ºF or until golden brown, cool and cut in slices of 8 x 3 cm and 2 cm high. For the ganache, cook 450 g cream with the glucose and trimoline. Pour the mixture over the chocolate and add the rest of the cream. Mix well and cool for twelve hours. Then whip it as whipping cream. For the sauce, caramelize the sugar, deglaze with water, add the cocoa, salt and orange juice and let cook for another two minutes. Strain through a sieve, boil again and dissolve the chocolate in it. Mix the rest of the ingredients, let cool and spin. For the granité, dissolve the sugar and chicory in the coffee and prepare as a granité. Create thin layers of génoise, puff pastry, ganache and the small waffle. Finish with the granite, sorbet and sauce.

## Honey jelly with nuts and apple chutney

*For 4 people:* 1 liter water, 200 g honey, deep-fried pasta.
*For the honey jelly:* 200 g honey syrup, 800 g water, 30 g honey,
4 sheets of gelatin.
*For the nut crunch:* 160 g egg white, 100 g flour, 60 g sugar,
60 g nut powder.
*For the apple chutney with dried fruits:* 200 g apple chunks,
60 g dried apricots, 60 g dried figs, 60 g raisins soaked in rum,
40 g lemon juice, 2 star anise.
*For the nut dough:* 125 g egg white, 40 g sugar, 125 g nut powder,
100 g icing sugar, 20 g flour.
*For the honey ice cream:* 500 g whole milk, 400 g egg yolk,
125 g cream, 75 g honey.

For the jelly, heat water, dissolve the pre-soaked gelatin in it, add the rest
of the ingredients and set aside. For the nut crunch, mix the sugar with
egg whites and add the flour. Pipe thin strings on a silpat, sprinkle with
nut powder and bake in the oven at 170°C/338°F until golden brown.
For the chutney, caramelize the apples in honey, add the fruits and other
ingredients and cook for a few minutes. For the nut dough, beat egg
whites with sugar, add the icing sugar and beat until stiff. Carefully blend
the nut powder and flour with the egg whites and bake at 240°C/465°F
or until golden brown. For the honey ice cream, combine the ingredients,
let set and put in ice cream machine. For the granité, mix water and
honey and freeze. Pour the honey jelly on a plate and let gel. Stack the nut
dough and chutney together and serve with ice cream and granité, nut
crunch and deep fried pasta.

137

## Baba with little fruit towers

*For the baba:* 800 g flour, 80 g salt, 280 g butter, 35 g yeast, 35 g honey, 1 kg eggs.

*For the baba syrup:* 1 liter water, 500 g sugar.

*For the sorbet:* 1000 g water, 500 g sugar, zest of 1 orange, zest of 1 lemon, Malibu, coulis of melon, strawberry and coconut.

*For the herb syrup:* 1200 g water, 100 g sugar, zest of 1 orange, 3 chamomile flowers, 5 g gelatin, different coarse herbs.

*For the honey tuille:* 120 g honey, 120 g sugar, 40 g flour, 40 g butter.

*For the little fruit tower:* melon, kiwi, brunoise of poached pineapple and poached pear.

For the baba, make a dough of flour, yeast and honey. Add salt and one egg at a time. Once the dough starts to loosen from the bowl, replace dough hook with the butterfly tool and add pieces of butter until you have a smooth dough. Let the dough rest and fill a greased baking pan of 35 x 40 cm, as well as some small baking tins and let rise for 35 minutes. Bake at 180ºC/355ºF or until golden brown; take out of the forms and let rest overnight. For the syrup, cook the water and sugar and cool. For the little sorbet tower, make a syrup of water, sugar and zests, make the coulis to 18ºB and spin. Create a little tower with the sorbets on a slice of baba, pipe some chocolate layers in between. For the herb syrup, boil the water and the ingredients and let simmer for one hour. Dissolve the pre-soaked gelatin in the mixture, pass through a sieve and set aside. For the tuilles, heat the honey to 40ºC/104ºF, mix with the sugar, butter and flour, spread on a silpat and bake at 180ºC/355ºF. Cut strips out of the tuille and create spirals. Serve the little tower with honey tuille and herb syrup. For the little fruit tower, use the ingredients and create a little tower in a fluted glass. Garnish with fresh fruit and Malibu, rum or kirsch.

## French toast with strawberries

*For 4 people:* powder made of dried strawberries,
200 ml strawberry juice.
*For the French toast:* 4 slices of brioche, 2 eggs, 2 cl kirsch,
brown sugar, 50 g crème d'aube, 16 strawberries, 50 g butter.
*For the fresh strawberries:* 10 strawberries, sugar, 10 mint leaves.
*For the milkshake:* 330 ml cream, 330 ml milk, 330 g ice-cubes
infused with strawberries.

Cut 16 strawberries in pieces and sauté in butter. Cut the brioche in
slices. Dip them in eggs that have been slightly beaten and fry in butter
and a bit of sugar. Serve the strawberries on the toast and drizzle with
crème d'aube. Cut fresh strawberries in slices and put some sugar and
thin slices of mint on top. For the milkshake, mix the cream, milk and ice
cubes to a foam. Fill each glass with strawberry juice and pour milkshake on top. Serve the fresh strawberries on a spoon with the toast and
milkshake.

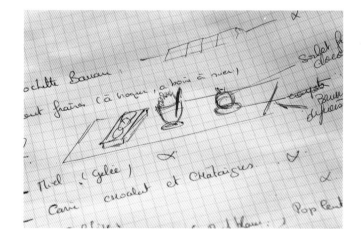

# Parfaits

A parfait is not just another ice cream invented for people who do not want a machine or cannot afford it. A description of parfait can be found in many old books. We go deeper into the old recipes and give them a modern twist.

## Urbain Dubois

The extensive book of this master dated in 1856 does not mention a parfait, but does mention the plombière. We therefore conclude that the parfait didn't exist in the mid- nineteenth century.

## Jules Gouffé

This teacher of Auguste Escoffier is as far as we know the first one who introduced the parfait in his book. This was in 1882. What Gouffé calls a parfait, is actually a plombière. The recipe is old, but the name is new.

*Faites torréfier 2 hectos de café;*
*Faites bouillir 12 décilitres de crème dans laquelle vous ferez infuser le café pendant 1 heure;*
*Mettez dans une casserole 12 jaunes d'oeufs et 2 hectos de sucre;*
*Faites lier sur le feu et passez à l'étamine;*
*Sanglez une sorbetière, puis un moule à parfait;*
*Mettez la crème dans la sorbetière et faites-la prendre en la travaillant avec la spatule; lorsq'elle commence à prendre, ajoutez 1 demi-décilitre de sirop de 32 degrés;*
*Continuez à travailler l'appareil; lorsque le sirop est bien mêlé, ajoutez encore 1 démi-décilitre de sirop, puis 8 décilitres de crème fouettée bien ferme;*
*Loulez dans le moule à parfait, couvrez et sanglez;*
*Au bout de 2 heures, démoulez sur une serviett*

Roast 200 g coffee. Bring 1200 ml of cream to a boil and infuse with the coffee for one hour. Put 12 egg yolks and 200 g sugar in a pan and stir with a spatula until it thickens. Sangleer* the ice cream machine, pour in the cream and work it with a spatula. As soon as it starts to thicken add 50 ml syrup of 32º. Keep stirring the mixture, add another 500 ml syrup and 800 ml strongly whipped cream. Pour in a parfait form, cover and sangleer. Freeze for 2 hours, release from the form and place on a serviette.

*Sangleer method :. Before electrical cooling and freezers were invented one used to sangleer which is cooling with ice and salt, salt being responsible for the lowering of temperature. Chefs used to be real craftsmen. In the old days it was so natural to add warm cream to egg yolks that Gouffé doesn't even mention that in his book. The reason we have to add the syrup in two portions is to prevent the mixture from getting too hot and losing its thickness.

The parfait au café from the book of Escoffier

# Auguste Escoffier

In 1902 August Escoffier is very brief in his French language book. He claims that the name parfait "was used only for parfait café and has become a common name for uncovered commercial ice cream, made on the basis of a bombe preparation with one perfume." This master hit the nail on the head, because the making of a parfait is almost the same as making a bombe, except for a few minor details. With this theory, says Escoffier, "we don't have to limit ourselves to a parfait café, but we can make the parfait with vanilla, chocolate or praliné." A bombe preparation is a foamy composition, created by beating egg yolks and syrup, finished with whipped cream. The only difference is that the bombe is covered with heavy cream.

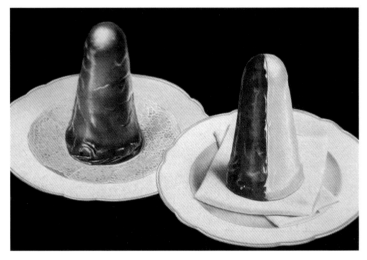

The parfait from the book L'Art Culinaire Moderne

# Prosper Montagné

L'Art Culinaire Moderne of Larousse 1936, written by Prosper Montagné, explains:

### LES PARFAITS

*Sortes de glaces très légères, d'une composition spéciale et qui ne nécessistent pas de sorbetière. L'appareil est préparé dans une terrine et mis directement dans un moule. Placer 2 1/2 à 3 heures dans la glace salée.*

This is a very light ice cream made without an ice cream machine. The composition is prepared in a terrine and immediately put in a mold. This is placed in salted ice for 2 ½ - 3 hours.

## Parfait au café

*Proportions: 200 gr. de sucre, 1 déci de café très fort, 8 jaunes d'oeufs, 3/4 de litre de crème fouettée.*

*Cuire le sucre, avec le café, au filé. Verser alors doucement ce sirop bouillant sur les jaunes d'oeufs en les rémuant. Fouetter le mélange jusqu'à ce qu'il soit complètement froid. Mélanger la crème fouettée et verser l'appareil dans un moule à parfait (moule à glace en forme de pain de sucre, fermant hermétiquement). On mastique le couvercle avec du beurre et on sangle pendant 3 heures. Nota. - On peut églement faire des farfaits à la vanille, au chocolat, au praliné, etc.*

*Ingredients: 200 g sugar, 100 ml very strong coffee, 8 egg yolks, 750 ml whipped cream.*

Boil sugar and coffee au filé. Pour the warm syrup on the egg yolks stirring continuously. Keep beating the egg yolks until they are cold. Add the whipped cream and pour in a parfait mold (a form like a sugar bread with an airtight lid). Put lid on with butter, making it airtight and place in ice and salt for 3 hours. This parfait can also be made with vanilla, chocolate or praliné.

Note: au filé means a temperature between 106-110C/220-230°F. In the past one would put his finger in cold water, then in syrup and then again in water. When you could make a thread of 5 mm thickness with the syrup, the temperature was au filé.

# Curnonsky

In 1953, the famous culinary journalist Curnonsky wrote:

## Parfait au café ou à la vanille

*Mélanger un demi-litre de pâte à bombe, au parfum choisi, à 6 dl de crème fouettée vanillée. Verser la composition dans un moule uni de forme conique et haute; bien remplir le moule; couvrir d'un papier blanc, puis du couvercle. Couper le papier qui dépasse et luter le couvercle et le moule avec beurre ou saindoux, afin que l'eau salée du sanglage ne s'introduise pas dans le moule.*
*Pour ce faire, veiller à ce que l'eau salée n'arrive jamais à hauteur du haut du moule. On vide cette eau et on resserre le sanglage.*
*In faut toujours sangler un parfait aussitôt qu'il est moelé; autrement, la crème peut se décomposer et égoutter du petit-lait qui se déposerait au fond du moule.*

Mix half litre of pâte à bombe with your choice of flavour and 600 ml whipped cream, infused with vanilla. Pour in a conical unrippled mold.

Fill to the top, cover with waxfree paper and close the lid with butter or lard, so that the salt cannot get inside. When making a parfait, one should always use the sangleer method so that the cream will not separate and leak whey to the bottom. (In the past the cream was obviously of a different quality)

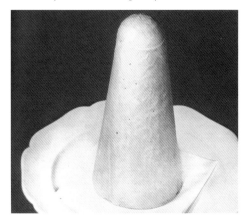

Parfait from the book L'Art Culinaire Français

## L'Art Culinaire Français

This book from 1957 by Falmmarion is short and forceful, although it seems that it came directly from Escoffier. Fortunately this book had another recipe that we hadn't seen before.

### *Parfait Balmoral*

*Faire un sirop avec 300 grammes de sucre, trois quarts de litre d'eau et une gousse de vanille. Mettre ce sirop en ébullition. Faire griller très fortement 300 grammes de noisettes et les jeter chaudes dans le sirop. Couvrir et retirer du feu pendant un quart d'heure. Passer au chinois et réserver dans un poêlon, mouiller les noisettes d'un verre d'eau et les remettre au feu, afin les laver du sirop et extraire tout le parfum de noisette, passer ce jus et le joindre au premier sirop. Cuire ce sirop très épais. Faire refroidir et mélanger à un demi-litre de crème fouettée. Sangler comme tout glace, servir avec sauce chocolat.*

Make syrup with 300 g sugar, 750 ml water and one vanilla bean and bring to a boil. Thoroughly roast 300 g hazelnuts and add them to the syrup. Take off the heat and let sit for 15 minutes covered. Push mix through a fine mesh sieve and set aside in a saucepan. Dampen the hazelnuts with a glass of water and put back on the burner so that all the flavour goes in the sugar. Drain the liquid, add to reserved syrup in the saucepan and boil again reducing it to a thick mass. Cool and add 500 ml whipped cream.

This is the first time we have seen a parfait where the thickness comes from syrup. No egg yolks were used although we read the recipe over and over because we couldn't believe it. We will try this again in the future but assume that the result will be sticky and greasy.

## Paul Bocuse

We move to 1976. Paul Bocuse has just moved away from the heavy kitchen classics and the entire culinary world holds its breath. In his book La Cuisine du Marché, which was published this year, he explained the parfait in great detail and wrote almost two full pages on the subject. The basic recipe he describes is from Escoffier: 1 ltr syrup, 32 egg yolks and 1 ltr whipped cream. But subsequently we see that a new era has started. Bocuse writes: *"La pratique moderne a appliqué à cette composition différants parfums. Je me bornerai à conseiller l'adjonction de 3 cuillerées à potage de pralin aux amandes broyé et tamisé par litre de parfait."* In modern times we can possibly use different perfumes. I would advise to add 2 soup spoons of praliné and blanched almonds to 1 ltr parfait.

In addition he gives many examples of flavours that go well with a parfait, from orange to red berries and from banana to melon. He finishes his story: *"La plus grande fantaisie peut donc se donner libre cours dès l'instant que les règles du bon goût et l'harmonie des saveurs ne sont pas omises."* Use your fantasy freely as long as the rules for taste and harmony are not forgotten.

So really nothing has changed since 1976. Thank goodness.

Modern parfaits can have many forms, colours and flavours.

144

*Glacerie*

# Ice Cream Tarts

For our glacerie we have gone into the world of ice cream tarts, and a visit to Huize van Wely, the most famous pâtisserie shop in the Netherlands that is also an educational institution for young students.

For many years Pieter Booij and his chef Adriaan van Haarden have been at the helm of this renowned establishment. We were happy to meet Pascal Aprahamian, who has worked here for over twenty years. An ice cream tart can be made with many kinds of ice cream: heavy cream, sorbets and parfaits. However it is difficult to create different shapes or forms with ice cream. On this visit we were shown two different tarts: the Fraise Bombe and the Victoria ice cream tart. Pascal explained the rules. He told us that working with the best and freshest products will enhance the taste of the ice cream. We couldn't agree more.

### The Fraise Bombe

To start Pascal advises us to find a spot close to a good freezer. The bombes used are made of thin steel and put in the freezer for a few minutes to get very cold. The bombe will be created with three layers of ice cream, starting with vanilla ice cream. Using a spatula the bombe is coated with just 3mm of ice cream. This is important so that the next layer will easily stick to it.
Pascal: "If I would start right away with a thick layer of ice cream it would collapse and we also prevent air bubbles this way. We let this layer freeze well, before we start with a second layer." You don't have to start with vanilla ice cream. There are more than enough possibilities and combinations. When the first layer has been well frozen it is time for the next vanilla ice cream layer. The inside of the bombe is prepared to get a smooth surface and then gets a thicker layer. The bombe is put back in the freezer again before the next layer goes on. This is a melon sorbet, which is made into a thick layer. Pascal uses his apron to rotate the bombes. "This is because my hands would be too warm and could touch the ice cream. Rotation of the bombes is not easy and needs a lot of practice. It is difficult because the thickness of the layers have to be the same, otherwise it would show when you cut the tart." Of course we understand that it would not be easy to hold bombes that are −22ºC/-7ºF in your bare hands! The last layer is a strawberry sorbet. To avoid air bubbles this layer is piped into the bombe. The piping bag and tip have first been put in the freezer, as Pascal makes sure that everything is ice cold. The bottom is smoothed out and then covered with a layer of moscovich biscuit that serves as the base for the tart.

## The Loosening of the Bombes and the Finish

Once the bombes have been well frozen, the task is to loosen them. This has to be done with a precision that needs a lot of experience. Pascal: "If a bombe is not cold enough, it will not loosen. The water temperature is also very important. The biscuit cannot become wet." Skillfully the bombes are immersed in a basin of warm water, about 50°C/120°F. Once Pascal feels that the bombes start to loosen he inverts them onto a plate. Then the tarts are frozen again while we prepare for the finishing.

This time they used a jelly, but it could also have been a ganache, a chocolate glaze or velvety chocolate. They start again with a very thin layer, this time of whipped cream, which forms the base for the jelly. The whipped cream is evenly distributed over the tart and has been slightly tinted so it will enhance the colour of the jelly. Once again the tarts go back in the freezer. In the meantime, the jelly is at the perfect temperature. "The jelly is critical. If that is not perfect we have to start all over with the whipping cream." The jelly Pascal uses is around 25°C/77°F. He glazes the bombes with a big spoon full of jelly. When the tart comes out of the freezer, it is garnished with almond wafers.

## The Victoria Ice Cream Tart

Next is the Victoria tart. This is built within a ring. First they start with a strip of polyprop. This strip not only makes it easier to loosen the tart but also prevents it from drying out. The inside of the ring is layered with small pieces of biscuits. Pascal explains that there are many possibilities to fill the tart: "We can use parfaits as was described in an earlier Pastry and Dessert magazine, but also compôtes, confitures and fruits. It is important that these don't harden too much in the freezer, so they add alcohol to the compôtes and use candied fruits." The first layer of ice cream is piped in. This starts in the corners to avoid air bubbles. After freezing a second layer is piped in, in this case raspberry sorbet. Pascal uses a very nice technique, with a moon shaped scraper to scoop equal depths that will give the top a different colour than the sides. Pascal emphasizes that the edges have to be very clean, otherwise the colours would mix with each other and spoil the beautiful effect. The last layer is a pear sorbet. Starting in the centre the tart is leveled smooth. A clear jelly is poured over the tart, which is evenly distributed in a circular motion. The air bubbles are removed by tapping the mould and the tart is garnished with a small great looking flower piece made of marzipan.

Pascal: " Making ice cream tarts is a joy and the applications are endless. Escoffier describes seventy-six varieties! One more tip: don't forget to take the tart out of the freezer one hour before you serve it."

Thanks Pascal!

# a visit to Nancy

## Under the green beam

The industrial environment is not very welcoming, but once you have arrived downtown in this old city of Eastern France, you can immediately feel a difference. The center is rich in eighteenth-century architecture, with heritage buildings that reveal grand status. But the heritage mixes at some spots with buildings of modern technology, showing that residents here do live in the twenty-first century. Just like everyone else who visits Nancy, we are magnetically drawn to Place Stanislas with its famous golden arches. The mayor has had this square beautifully restored. There are many golden arches, so that the statue of this distinguished famous local person Stanislas can be seen from every angle. While we are visiting, the Christmas holidays are starting, which is emphasized by the beautiful festive lights.

In Nancy, everything evolves around Leszcynski Stanislas who lived from 1677 to 1766. He was the king of Poland, whose daughter married Louis XV. With that union, he became Duke of Bar and Lotharingen and father-in-law of the king, which gave him access to enormous financial wealth. He spent much money on the restoration of Nancy, which was up until then a city of poverty. He built palaces, created parks and encouraged art in the streets. This made him the hero of Nancy, and that is still the case. You can't walk in too many places in Nancy without seeing this historical figure celebrated in one way or another. But we are here for the pâtisserie and confiserie. Nancy is very famous for its macaroons and bergamot (pear shaped citrus fruit). Although the macaroons of Nancy have a great reputation in France, we don't find them appealing. They are made much the same way as anywhere else and baked on edible paper. The bergamot is more interesting, because you only see this confiserie in Nancy. The bergamot is a citrus fruit that doesn't grow around Nancy, but in the Calabria region in southern Italy. Why then bergamot in Nancy? Stanislas, our hero, loved this fruit, so every person in Nancy loves them. In those days, a new candy culture evolved around the bergamot. Every local pâtissier creates his own version. Nancy also seems to be known for its pâtisserie with mirabelle, a regional plum, but we didn't see much of that during our visit. As in every city, each pâtissier has his own specialties, which he keeps secret as much as possible.

## Nathalie Lalonde

The shop-with-atelier, which employs eight staff, was started by the great-grandfather of the current owner. In 1975 the store moved from the center of Nancy to a location with enough space to expand.

The chef-pâtissier is the friendly Didier Tussaulx, a man who works at least seventeen hours a day. It shows in his eyes. In contrast, the owner is there about 15 minutes a day; she doesn't have the dark circles under her eyes. Didier introduces us to his products. He is very proud of his christaline, the specialty of the house. He mixes marzipan with gianduja (a sweet chocolate containing about 50% hazelnut, almond, or any other nut paste), fruit puree (of pistachio extract) and colouring. He turns these into flattened little balls, which he dips in sugar syrup. Because of their crunchy layer, they have a nice bite; the taste is fresh and fruity. Another specialty is the charlestine, a praline that is dipped twice in glace royal. We are not crazy about that one. More interesting are the mirabelles. Jellied starch is marinated in Mirabelle plum brandy; then shapes of small plums are formed and covered all around with marzipan and sprayed with the right colour. The balance between the strong liquor and the marzipan is very pleasant. Only in the winter does Didier bake a chocolate cake that has a spicy taste with a good balance between chocolate, spices and large pieces of dried tropical fruits.

## André Thiébaut

This shop has a tea-room and a staff of nine people. André values the seasons and only wants to work with quality ingredients. He is very proud to be a member of the Relais Dessert International. When we ask him what his specialty is, he also brings up the macaroon. "But my macaroons are very special, because I add a little bit of honey." What we find even more interesting is his Pavé de la place, which resembles the cobblestones of Place Stanlislas, fictitious of course. André makes his pavés equal parts almonds, hazelnut and sugar, which he caramelizes and then grinds. He mixes this powder with cocoa butter and feuillantine. With this he creates these little pavés and takes them through a mixture of cocoa powder and ground feuillantine. This is the best truffle we have ever had. When you bite into it, you get three tasting sensations: a dry fondant, a touch of hard caramel and a crunchy feuillantine. At Thiébaut we also find bergamot candies, although we find them a little too strong for our taste.

# The sugar doctor

We enter the slightly old fashioned shop, of which the outside is painted in a pleasing pink. A man who looks as if he just stepped out of a painting of the thirties welcomes us. We give him our pink business card and immediately he has a big smile of recognition on his face. "You are like me. Do you know why I painted my store in pink? Pink is the colour of people who dare. Rose est ose!" (ose means: people who have the guts). He takes us to his workshop and shows us his candied glasswork, which doesn't seem like glasswork. "Do you know why this colour is green?", he asks. We shake our head. "It is the green beam of the cathedral". We happen to know that the green beam from the cathedral has to do

with alchemy of the Middle Ages. In those days people believed that you could make gold under a green beam. "Pâtissiers are a bit like alchemists, because we also keep our recipes secret". The pink paint on the façade, the green colour of the beam, what else do you expect? This becomes clear very soon when we ask him to demonstrate his glasswork. Jean-François Adam replies: "Oh no, I won't have time for that, because I am not just a pâtissier, but also do magnetism and I am a healer." Now we know what he is all about. The man is probably looking right through us, and discovering all kinds of diseases we are not aware of! We go back to the topic of glasswork. Our pâtissier started to make these sugar pieces

  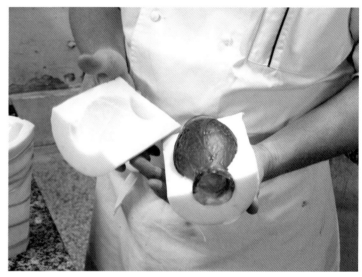

in 1990; this was for the agriculture salon in Paris. These were made from glucose, fondant sugar and of course colouring agents. He had special silicone forms made for this, imprints of authentic glassworks from the Nancy School, an early French suggestion-centered school of psychotherapy founded in 1866. However he does not sell these creations, because they don't stay beautiful. "But I do have two sugar vases, which are still beautiful after many years," says Jean-François. "I checked them with a pendulum and indeed, they are still giving positive rays." We realize that we should not laugh, because our host would end the conversation immediately. So we keep our lips tight!

Jean-François bought this store in 1983. The previous owner committed suicide after a bankruptcy. "I heard that later. One of my students told me that he sensed something. Later I understood why". Now the story takes an interesting turn. "When I arrived here people thought I was crazy. What would I do here, in a shop that was often empty, there were no customers and everyone went bankrupt? I had no doubt, because I felt that all negative energy could be turned into positive energy. I was lucky, which the previous owners didn't know, because I took over a trade mark, that went back to 1907, which was Saint-Epvre." The trademark turned out to be a tart.

# The Tart Saint-Epvre

Saint-Epvre was the seventh bishop of Nancy and gave his name to the square where the pâtisserie is established. Early in the twentieth century the store was taken over by a pâtissier of Tours. It became obvious that he could not make macaroons; the dough failed because of a mistake in the recipe. He added a bit of egg white and more adjustments and suddenly something new was created. In 1907 he put his own trademark on it. Jean-François thinks that he is not only the owner of this trademark but also of this recipe. Anyone who dares to use the name Saint-Epvre or even tries to make the same recipe is in for a big fight. Jean-François: "My lawyer has already written over one-hundred-fifty letters and some people are faced with a court case. I have won three cases already." Every time Jean-François goes to his lawyer, he takes a tart with him. Then he says: "It is this we fight for." He says his lawyer is happy with a client who not only pays him an honorarium, but also gives him a tart. He does not want to share his recipe with us, that is a secret. Without being an alchemist, we assume the recipe is as follows: A meringue with small pieces of almond and nougatine is piped in the form of chipolata (the spiral of life!) and baked in the oven. Between two sheets of meringue, put vanilla butter cream and powder ground from pieces of bergamot candies. The sides of the tart are covered with dried ground old meringue. The tart goes in the cooler for four days before it is sold. The cooler is divided in four compartments. We don't dare to ask if the number four is symbolic.

# Bergamote de Nancy

The candies that you see everywhere in Nancy are also seen in abundance at Jean-François Adam. He is very willing to show us how they are made, as there are no secrets involved here. "The secret is in the essence". Sugar and glucose are boiled to 162°C/323°F, and after a lot of hissing and sputtering, the essence of the bergamot is added. The pâtissier keeps stirring in one direction, which is to the right. The mixture is poured on a baking sheet and is cut within 3 minutes with a pizza cutter. After it has cooled off, it will be broken into small squares. The only difference between these and the other candies we have seen is the colour. These ones are slightly green. Jean-François: "Most of my colleagues boil their sugar at 160°C/320°F, the 2 to 3 degrees difference gives it another colour." Also, the bergamote essence is a very deep green. We have to say that Jean-François's bergamots are the best in Nancy. At least compared to all the ones we have tried. We leave with full energy on our way back home.

It is fall in the hills of the South of France. The last vestiges of the summer sun warm the fresh morning air. A light wind stirs the leaves of the chestnut trees, which rustle as the spiky outer shells of the nuts fall to the ground. A new season has begun.

# The Chestnut

During this time of year, French villagers go for their Sunday afternoon stroll with a plastic bag in their hands. They're about to take part in a yearly event nobody wants to miss. The forests are full of chestnut trees. The roads look as if they are covered with snow because of the white flesh of the broken chestnuts. Each tree produces large or small fruits and everyone knows his or her own favorite tree. Although this harvest is a pleasant diversion for many, we also observe a few professional hunters, who are quite particular in their search for quality product. In the middle ages, the chestnut was the number one food source for the people of southern France. Grains were rare, because the land wasn't very fertile, but the chestnuts provided abundant food energy in an era in which there was little else to eat the rest of the year. Late into the nineteenth century, this still was the case in many regions, until the introduction of the potato from the New World. Every suitable piece of land was planted with chestnut trees. Those bad times are now behind them, but the chestnut trees remain. Most forests in the south are covered with chestnut trees, with the tame (sweet) kind of chestnut, as we call it. The current ubiquitous nature of the tree owes not only from the plantings, but also to the tendency of the tree to spread 'offspring' as part of its natural reproductive cycle.

### Three hundred varieties

The chestnut has made a comeback over the last few years, where people have started to eat it the way it was in the past. During the harvest, the chestnuts are eaten raw or boiled, or roasted on the stove or a wooden fire. In order to preserve them they have to be dried first. This is done in a little stone hut, which is called cleda or clède. This little hut has two floors with a space underneath to light a small fire. This drying process takes six to seven weeks. The chestnut is peeled with a tool called a pisaire. A soup, called bajanat, can be made with the dried and peeled fruits. Or you can put it through a mill and make flour for baking.

Not only is the fruit used, the leaves can be used for animal feed and the wood can be used for to create hardwood floors, furniture, wooden stairs, beehives and so on. Chestnut wood does not rot easily and is therefore very popular as a building material.

It is the peak of harvest time when we meet Christian and Sabine Clermon in the little village of Les Eperelles. Their chestnut forest of 28 hectares produces 6000 kilos of crop. They keep 1500 kilos for the production of cognac, chestnut cream and chestnut purée. For this they use two kinds of chestnuts: the figarette and the pellegrine. Dried chestnuts and chestnut flour are made from the rabaire, comballe and carbide. Christian tells us that there are more than 300 varieties of chestnuts. The trees grow at elevations from 200 to 800 meters above sea level and can live for 200 years. They begin to produce nuts between the third and sixth years. The plantation needs to be worked through the whole year. The old trees get cut; then young trees are planted. The soil and ground around the tree have to be kept free of debris so they can put a net around the trunk at harvest time. Some of the land has such steep terrain that a net is impossible to use, so there the chestnuts are collected by hand.

### Châtaigne or Marron?

We have never understood the difference between a chestnut and a marron. Everyone has a different explanation. Fortunately we get the right answer from Christian. In the brown shell of the original chestnut are two or three fruits. This is the wild kind, which is called bouscas, mostly of bad quality. In the past centuries, researchers started to cultivate this to try and create a chestnut with one fruit only. Besides the already mentioned different kind of chestnuts, these ones are called dauphine, bouche rouge, bouche de Bétizac and peyrejonte. It is not true that these chestnuts just give one fruit; they have a mélange of different ones. But the chestnuts that really produce only one fruit are called

marrons. These are the really large chestnuts. If you see a jar that says purée de marron, you are most likely fooled. Why would anyone use the best and largest chestnuts to make a purée? Sabine shows us how to best peel a chestnut. You have to cut the chestnut in a special way with a special little knife, called the serpe or serpette, and then put it in boiling water for a few minutes. As soon as the outer shell opens up and you can see the white flesh emerging, take it out of the water. She tells us to do this bit by bit so that the chestnuts cannot completely cool off, which makes peeling more difficult. The best way to keep the chestnuts fresh? Sabine prefers to keep them in a cool spot. Most farmers keep them in a pot filled with some not too wet sand. It is essential that the fruits do not dry out.

In the boundless southern France countryside, farmers continue to use the chestnut. The basic recipes are centuries old and the knowledge is passed on from mother to daughter. Here are some of the most authentic recipes:

### Châtaignes Blanchies
**Blanched Chestnuts**

Take one or two kilos of chestnuts and remove the outside layer with a sharp knife. Put in light salted boiling water, which will bring out the sweetness. Keep the pot tightly covered. After boiling another eight to ten minutes, the second peel should be easily removed. Remove the second peel with a déboiradour or deiviroli (a small wooden tool, consisting of two little sticks glued together) making sure that you do not damage the flesh of the fruit. Rinse in cold water and put them on two blanched cabbage leaves.

Put in a pan with a bit of water, cover the pan tightly with a lid, and let steam for about 30-45 minutes. The danger is that the cabbage burns and that the chestnuts get a smoky taste. An alternative method is to use potatoes in the bottom of the pan, but the chestnuts cannot touch the bottom. The farmers eat this sprinkled with sweet wine. Some eat it with butter on top and add a shot of sweetened milk to it.

### Châtaignes sous la Cendre
**Chestnuts under Ash**

For this, use beautiful round chestnuts, which are the marons. Cut the two skins over the whole length. Put the chestnuts under hot ash from an open fire until they split open. Farmers do this during cold winter nights as they gather around the fire, telling stories and reliving memories. Of course this goes together with a glass of white wine from the most recent harvest. The chestnuts can also be grilled in the oven or in a pot with holes in the bottom.

### *La Compôte de Marrons entiers*
#### Compôte with whole Marrons

Start with 750 grams of round marrons and remove the outside layer and the second peel. Rinse under cold water and gently boil with a bit of water and a vanilla bean. Make sure the marrons don't break. Drain and put into a bowl with the vanilla bean. In the meantime, make some syrup from water and icing sugar. After the syrup has boiled for a few minutes, pour it over the maroons and let rest for a few hours, stirring from time to time so that the marrons confit in the syrup. Put the marrons in a pot, mix with their own sauce and glaze with a bit of caramel. Some farmers do it differently; they put it first under ash and then make confit in vanilla syrup. This is nice in-between meal snack.

### *Gâteau de Châtaigne*
#### Chestnut Tart

This is quite a heavy dessert, which starts with a Massepain du Périgord, although there are no almonds in this, so it is not really marzipan.
The oven cannot be opened while this tart is baking, as is possible with other cakes. Chestnut tarts don't like peeping Toms!
Separate 6 eggs. Mix the egg yolks with 6 tablespoons of icing sugar and whip until homogenized and fluffy. Then add 6 tablespoons of potato flour or wheat flour and
1½ tsp orange blossom water. Whisk the egg whites until very stiff and slowly blend it with the egg yolk mixture. Grease a tart form with plenty of butter, pour the mixture in and bake in a tempered oven. This tart becomes an attractive soufflé and will have a beautiful color on the outside. Sprinkle with icing sugar. Cut the tart horizontally in half so you will get two round cakes. Sprinkle with some eau de vie, which has been mixed with water and icing sugar. Make a chestnut purée, same as for the compôte. Also make a sugar syrup and, as soon as that is boiling, add to the warm purée. Blend 2 egg yolks with a bit of (home made) vanilla sugar and add to purée. Once it is cooled off, spread this mixture on one of the cake halves and cover with the other half. Pour a chocolate glaze over the top (do this by heating 1 tablespoon of icing sugar, a little bit of water, and 25 g chocolate). Add a bit of butter, cool, and spread the glaze on top with a warm knife. Put in the oven for one minute so the choco-late becomes glossy. Instead of crème de châtaigne, you can make confiture de châtaigne, mixed with egg yolk. That tart will be done faster.

## La Confiture de Châtaigne

Can be eaten any time of the day and also be used for tarts. Peel the chestnuts and boil with a vanilla bean until well done and they fall apart. Push the mass through a sieve or purée with a passevite (a tool used for mashing vegetables) Make a syrup (3 parts sugar for 4 parts purée, some vanilla and water), bring to a boil and add purée, stirring until it gets the right consistency. The confiture should have the colour of a chestnut, not light beige. Fill canning jars with this confiture.

## Chestnut Bread

*Yields 10 loaves of bread of 150 g:* 700 g all purpose flour, 300 g chestnut flour, 600 g water, 20 g yeast, 20 g salt.

Mix both flours with salt at room temperature. Add the yeast and let it mix for 20 minutes at a moderate speed. Let the dough rest for one hour, create balls of 150 g each, put on a baking sheet lined with parchment paper and let rise for a while. Put the loaves in a preheated oven of 250°C /480oC F and lower the oven temperature every 5 minutes by 10°C/50°F until it drops down to 200oC/390°F. The loaves should be ready in 30 minutes. The loaves will colour very quickly because of the natural sugar content of the chestnut flour. The loaves stay good for three to four days.

## Chestnut Florentines

*Ingredients:* 150 g sugar, 75 g chestnut flour, 3 egg yolks, 150 g almond powder, 5 drops of vanilla extract.

Beat the egg yolks with the sugar and the vanilla extract until it starts to look white. Add the flour and the almond powder and let rest for 20 minutes. Grease and flour a baking sheet and create florentines by flattening them with the use of a tablespoon. Bake in the oven at 170°C/340°F for 7 or 8 minutes. Keep in a tight container.

## Chestnut Meringue Tart

*For the dough:* 500 g chestnut flour, 12 g salt, 150 g butter, 1 egg, 50 g water
*For the chestnut crème:* 500 g chestnut purée, 75 g milk, 3 eggs, 75 g sugar, 5 g vanilla extract

Mix flour with butter and salt, add eggs and water, and let dough rest in the fridge for 20 minutes. Roll the dough out to 2 mm thick and line the bottom of the tart forms. Poke some holes in the dough with a fork. Mix the chestnut purée with the egg yolks, the milk and the vanilla. Beat the egg whites with the sugar and carefully mix with the chestnut mixture. Fill the tart forms and bake in the oven at 165°C/330°F for 35 to 45 minutes. Cool and remove from the forms. Prepare a meringue with 2 egg whites and 120 g sugar. Top tart with meringue and put under the salamander for a few minutes.

## Nut Crunch

*Ingredients:* 250 g icing sugar, 150 g chestnut flour, 7,5 g baking soda, 125 g unpeeled hazelnuts, 125 g unpeeled almonds, 100 g melted butter, 50 g crème fraîche, 5 g vanilla extract, egg yolk for glazing.

Grind the nuts with the sugar, the vanilla and the crème fraîche in the kitchen robot and add the melted butter; add flour and baking soda. Form a ball with the dough, cover with a towel, and let rest in the fridge for 15 minutes. Roll out the dough to 8 mm and coat with some beaten egg yolk. Bake in the oven at 210ºC/410ºF for 30 minutes. Lower the oven temperature every 10 minutes by 10ºC/50ºF. Let cool.

## Chestnut Candy Cake

*A cake form for 6-8 pieces:* 250 g chestnut flour, 250 g honey, 200 g lukewarm milk, 3 eggs, 15 g dry yeast, 2.5 g baking soda, 2.5 g salt, 5 g ground anise, 3 g ground cinnamon, 2 g ground cloves, peel of one orange.

Sieve flour with yeast and baking soda. Mix eggs with the honey. Add the milk, then the flour mix, and finish with all the spices and the cut orange peel. Make it into dough. Butter a cake pan and lay dough inside. Bake in the oven at 160ºC/320ºF for 35 minutes. Cover the cake with some wax paper to avoid discolouring.

## Chestnut Tart

*Ingredients:* 80 g sugar, 4 eggs, 100 g melted butter, 40 g olive oil, 50 g chestnut flour, 3 g baking soda, 40 g chestnut crumbles, 40 g chestnut purée.

Mix eggs and sugar in a food processor, add melted butter and olive oil. Then add the chestnut purée and let it mix for a few minutes. Sieve flour and baking soda and carefully add to the mixture. Line a round cake from with parchment paper and fill the pan with ¾ of the dough. Bake in the oven at 175ºC/350ºF for 30-40 minutes. Release from the form and let cool on a rack. Drizzle the tart with reduced chestnut syrup. The tart stays good for 3-4 days.

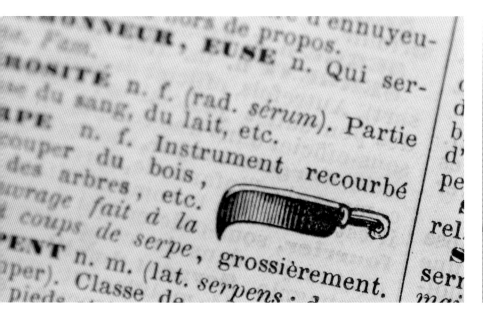

# Barbe à papa

*Cotton Candy
or Candy Floss*

The history of sugar spinning started centuries ago. When exactly isn't clear, but sugar spinning was well known before the 18th century. In those days one would twist two forks with caramel above an upside-down, greased bowl. The threads of caramel would become a ball that was used as decoration. At Easter it was used as a bird's nest, but was also beautifully displayed on a profiterole. That method is hardly used today. However, sugar spinning is now a trendy and retro piece of patisserie. We have seen it return on dessert trays in several top restaurants.

## The Inventors

There are several people who have claimed credit for the invention of spun sugar as a candy. What we know for sure is that the first electric sugar-spinning machine was patented on January 31st, 1899. John Warton and William Morrison from Nashville, Tennessee invented a machine which made it possible to spin sugar into silky threads by means of centrifugal power. A year later, Thomas Patton received a separate patent for the making of cotton candy. When Warton and Morrison introduced their machine, it became a revolution. It was even called a miracle of science. At that time the machines were not very reliable, but that changed in 1949 when sugar-spinning machines were modernized. Today these machines are used professionally for fun fairs, but you can also purchase them for home use. For a few dollars you can buy a little machine at any wholesaler and use them in restaurants and ice cream parlors. Just like the machines, the name itself has been revolutionized. Originally the name was fairy floss and the English called it candy cotton. Around 1908 it was called edible cotton in Western Europe. Americans are so enthralled with this candy every December 7th is the official Cotton Candy Day.

## The Practice

Cotton candy can be made in different colors and is always made with chemically made flavors. The problem with natural flavors is that the centrifugal power of the machine will reject anything that is a different weight than sugar. We discovered this the hard way, in our tasting kitchen. We literally tried everything, often with undesirable results. And yet we discovered some great inventions, which we pass on to you here.

## Sugar test

In our tasting kitchen we used a small household machine, brand-name Princess. It works the same as a professional machine (we assume that the production capacity of a professional machine will be higher), but in quality it makes little difference. We found some very tiny sugar drops in our spun sugar. They were hardly noticeable to the naked eye. The purpose of our experiment was to see if we could expand our boundaries. All sugars, sweeteners and a lot of other ingredients came straight out of our cupboard. Sugar that was too coarse for the machine was first pulverized.

Here are our first test results: We found, that next to granulated sugar, candy sugar gave by far the best result. We used 2 teaspoons in each test and tried every kind of sugar we could find:

*Granulated sugar:* The spun sugar rises to the top of the bowl easily. We could make two large sticks or 10 small ones.

*White caster sugar:* When we started with this kind of sugar, so much was thrown out of the machine we could only make one thin sugar stick.

*Icing sugar:* This sugar is unsuitable, nothing happened.

*Trehalose (Mycose sugar):* This sugar hardly rose to the top of the bowl, which meant that we couldn't even make half a stick.

*Dextrose:* Never use this one. We almost had to replace the machine!

*Fructose:* Also a problem here; no spun sugar. Many little bits were thrown out, which resembled glucose syrup.

*Jelly sugar:* Again the spun sugar really doesn't come to the top, so it is difficult to make a stick. The result is just one stick, but the taste is excellent: slightly sour and a bit lemony.

*Coarse candy sugar:* Unexpectedly, this one seems to be a winner. We pulverized the sugar a bit. The result was three beautiful strong spun sugar sticks with lots of volume.

*Cassonade sugar (brown sugar):* This sugar gives a white spin with drops of caramel. The threads are very sticky, the result low. Interesting caramel taste, though.

*Palm sugar:* This sugar makes a light brown spun sugar because of the caramel content. The result, however, is less than half a stick.

*Molasses:* Not at all workable.

*Raw cane sugar:* This sugar makes thin loose threads with a fluffy spin. Unfortunately, it made only one stick.

*Demerara Sugar:* At first the result looks great, but diminishes in volume very quickly. Makes a little less than one stick.

*Isomaltose (chemically induced sugar):* These pearls of sugar are no success in the machine. The spun threads are too hard to eat.

## Playing with the effects

It is not easy to add flavors to sugar. Not to worry, there are other ways to add flavor to your cotton candy. For instance, you can sprinkle a mixture of cinnamon and icing sugar on top, something that also has a surprising effect. You must sprinkle this just before it is to be eaten, as the spun sugar is very prone to collapsing. Beside spices, you can also create your own powders for example, by grinding candies and putting them through a sieve. This way we can create cotton candy with the taste of "Haagse Hopjes" (typical Dutch candy), Napoleon bonbons and little sugar hearts.

## Carnivalesque

We tried to sprinkle a powder on the threads while they were being spun in the machine. This only worked with very light products. That gave us the idea to shred colored candy paper and sprinkle it. This gives a very colorful carnival effect. This paper has to be shredded very fine otherwise it would not be pleasant to taste. We also tried freeze-dried herbs. That gave us some surprises as well. It's just a matter of experimenting...

## Each one on its own stick

Spun sugars are usually wrapped onto thin sticks. We discovered that the stick could play a role by itself. While you are eating cotton candy, the stick is very close to your nose. If you provide the little stick with some flavor, you can smell that while you eat. That gives the impression that the sugar itself has the flavor. There are different ways of making the little stick smell. For instance, you can marinate the stick, but we discovered an even faster technique. Immerse the top of the stick in glucose and use the sticky top to glue something on it. That can be a kind of powder, but even some spices or cress. We had surprising results with fleur de sel and with piment d'Espelette.

If you want to go one little step further you can attach something to the little stick. This will give a nice surprise right away. Think about products that go traditionally well with sugar, like a piece of seared foie gras or a strawberry. Strawberries and sugar are classic. By stabbing a dried strawberry on the little stick, surrounded by the sugar spin, you will add a surprising element to this theme.

Why all this fuss around candy floss? The answer is simple: these preparations can come in handy for yourself. The material costs almost nothing and the floss can be made in hardly any time at all. With this you can create a volume that can enrich your dessert creations and the restaurant patron seems to get a lot more value for his money. We also see possibilities in the ice cream parlor. Honestly, what child would not be enchanted with a little spun sugar added onto their ice cream?

P09

# Gérald Passédat
# Le Petit Nice

This hotel has a view of the Mediterranean, an incredible vista. Gérald Passédat is a 3 star Michelin chef and the undisputed phenomenon of Marseille. He learned the art of cooking from his father, who was also at the top of the gastronomic world. Together with his two chefs, Dennis Maillet and Philippe Moreno, Gérald creates desserts that are always technical marvels. The flavors are subtle and fluffy, always with an interesting play on textures.

www.petitnice-passedat.com

*Chocolate caramel cylinder with caramel-espuma*

*For the cylinder:* 250 g sugar, 125 g glucose, 90 g pure chocolate.
*For the chocolate stalk:* 180 g sugar syrup (1:1), 30 g glucose, 90 g cocoa powder.
*For the caramel espuma:* 1 litre cream, 250 g sugar, 10 egg yolks, 200 ml doused caramel.
*For the balsamic syrup:* 300 ml balsamic vinegar, 100 ml sugar syrup (1:1).

For the cylinder, cook sugar and glucose to 158°C/316°F, let cool slightly and mix the chocolate with the caramel. Pour the mixture on parchment paper and let cool a bit. Roll the caramel into a very thin layer, cut into slices of 5 x 10 cm and form into cylinders. For the chocolatestalk, mix all ingredients, pour in a piping bag and pipe very thin strings on a silpat. Bake in the oven at 170°C/340°F for 7 minutes. Make a crème anglaise with the cream, sugar and egg yolks. Mix this with the doused caramel and pour in a siphon. Cool and insert charger before use. For the balsamic syrup mix the vinegar and the syrup and reduce to half. Fill the cylinder with the espuma and stick a chocolate string in it. Serve with the balsamic syrup.

### Yeti made of milk foam and green apple

*For 4 people:* 1 granny smith apple.
*For milk foam:* 40 g milk, 20 g sugar syrup (1:1), ½ vanilla bean,
1 sheet of gelatin, 40 g ice-cold milk.
*For the apple jelly:* a granny smith apple, 70 g sugar syrup (1:1),
70 g water, 1 tb lemon juice, 0.25 g agar-agar, 1 tb apple liqueur,
green colouring.
*For the apple sorbet:* 90 g peeled apple, 70 g sugar syrup 30°B,
70 g trimoline, 5 g lemon juice.

Cut the apple in thin slices, roll them and let dry in the oven. For the milk foam: heat the milk, sugar syrup and vanilla bean. Dissolve the soaked gelatin in this mixture and let cool. Whisk the ice-cold milk to a foam and slowly add the other cooled milk mixture. For the jelly, peel the apple and cut in pieces. Cook this with the syrup, water and lemon juice and purée with a handheld blender. Add the agar-agar and the liqueur and delicately add some green coloring. Cook a bit longer and pour on a platter. Cool and cut little slices from it. For the sorbet, purée the apple pieces with syrup, trimoline and lemon juice. Let rest for a few hours and mix at high turbo speed. Set the sorbet aside in small cylinders. In a tall narrow glass, build layers of foam and jelly with the sorbet in the center. Serve with the apple chips and two balls of milk foam.

## Fruit pipettes in milk mousse

*For 4 people:* a thin slice of sponge cake.
*For the basil pipettes:* 250 g fondant, 125 g glucose, 1 bunch chopped basil.
*For the milk mousse:* 200 ml milk, 2 sheets of gelatin, zest of 1 lemon, 200 ml ice-cold milk.
*For the coulis:* 100 g mango pulp, 100 g peeled pear, 100 g peeled kiwi, 100 g raspberries or other fruit in season.
*For orange fizzy crackling powder:* the peel of one orange, 200 ml sugar syrup (1:1), 10 g crackling powder.

For the basil pipettes cook the fondant and glucose to 158°C/316°F and add the chopped basil. Pour on wax paper, let cool and roll out between 2 sheets of paper until it is very thin. Cut slices of 6 x 3 cm and make them in pipettes. Create little bottoms from the sponge cake for the pipettes. For the mousse, heat 200 ml milk, dissolve the soaked gelatin in this and let cool. Finely chop the zest of the lemon. Whip the ice-cold milk until foamy and slowly add the other already cooled milk. Add the lemon zest. Spoon the foam in tall narrow glasses and set aside to cool. For the coulis, purée all the fruits separately and fill the pipettes before serving. For the powder, peel the orange with a zester, blanch the peel three times and glaze in the sugar syrup. Let the glazed peel dry, grind in the mixer to make a powder and mix with the crackling crystals. Serve the fruit pipettes in the milk mousse. Sprinkle the foam with the orange crackling powder.

P09

## Crunchy cigarettes with a coffee stack

*For the coffee granité (granita):* 250 g coffee, 50 g sugar, 1 sheet of gelatin, 10 g whiskey.

*For tuile dough:* 250 g sugar, 2 eggs, 125 g egg white, 50 g melted butter, 80 g flour.

*For the milk cloud:* 200 g milk, 40 g icing sugar, 1 vanilla bean.

*For the coffee cloud:* 180 g coffee, 60 g sugar, 1 sheet of gelatin.

*For the coffee caramel:* 100 g sugar, 100 g coffee.

For the granité, heat the coffee and sugar, dissolve the soaked gelatin in it and add the whiskey. Create a granité with this mix. For the tuile dough, mix all the ingredients, pour and smooth out thinly on a silpat and bake in the oven at 170ºC/340ºF. Cut in slices of 10 x 3 cm and roll up like a cigarette. For the milk cloud, mix the milk, icing sugar and vanilla bean. Cool, and whisk up with a Frix Air (very high speed turbine mixer). For the coffee cloud, heat the coffee and the sugar, immerse the soaked gelatin and keep cool in a Frix beaker. Whisk to a foam before serving. For the coffee caramel, caramelize the sugar and douse with the coffee. Build a stack with the milk and coffee cloud and put granité in between. Serve the stack on the little cigarettes.

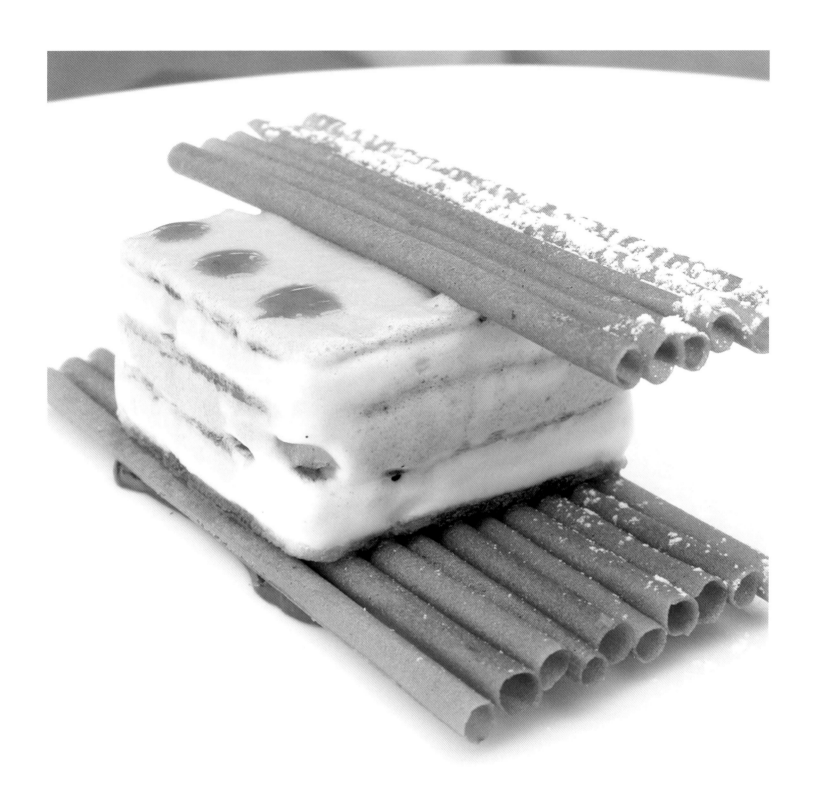

# London

We carefully planned our trip. However, it was clear that we had not realized how large this metropolitan city is; the locations we wanted to visit were sometimes far apart. A day-trip card with public transport was our saviour.

We are going to this big city full of anticipation, curious to find fun pastry shops, and traditional lemon curd and jelly pudding. We must have been a little too excited, because no matter where we looked, it was hard to find these cute shops; they seem to be passé in 2008. According to the pâtissiers we met, we would have to go to the English countryside. London is a very expensive city, which is why many small artisan bakeries had to leave, between the high rents and competition from the large commercial businesses. However, there are still many shops where we find croissants and buns and where we can also find our lemon curd. It is too bad that these have been taken over by pizzerias. Are we disillusioned? No, because at the pâtisserie department of the immensely huge Harrods store we find several of the delicacies we are looking for. Compared to Amsterdam or Brussels, London has only a few selected top pâtissiers. However, on our way we still find some kind of craftsmanship. For example, there is a wagon at the station which has Cornwall Pastry written on it in big letters. It is not sweet pastry but savory. The history of this pastry is fairly recent. In the labour environment of Cornwall, in the far corner of England, the women would bake this kind of pastry for their husband-miners. The pie dough was made with lard and filled with a hearty amount of vegetables and meat. They used the dough leftovers to make the initials of their husbands and put on top of the pies. Those pies would be lowered on a rope to go into the mines. The tradition continued and became known outside the mines. Some of the flavors are beef and Stilton, cheese and onions, lamb, and pieces of the classic roast beef, potatoes, onions and cabbage.

At another spot in London, under the Big Ben, we find Radar, a jolly immigrant who has been roasting and caramelizing nuts for over twenty-seven years. Radar does not want his picture taken, as he is an illegal immigrant. Of course we wouldn't want him to be deported, so we didn't take a picture. First he sautés the nuts in sunflower oil and then adds some sugar to give them a thin coating. Simplicity at its best! Illegal or not, the nuts are delicious and cheap. If you happen to be in that area in London, then do go to the London Eye, the Ferris wheel. It gives you a spectacular view of the entire city. Don't worry about rain or wind as the carts are closed in.

175

## Piccadilly

We arrive at Piccadilly, the street that merges with the intersection of the very clear neon and advertising signs. In this street we find a variety of pâtisserie stores. One is called Pâtisserie Valerie, a store where the business people quickly get their coffee and pastry before they go to work. This shop goes back to 1926 and was started by Italian immigrants. The specialty of the house is double chocolate cake. We continue our trip down the street. We are so happy that we don't have to go underground to take the metro and are able to walk to a nice passageway where our eyes catch a gold shop window with impressive towers made of macaroons. The name of the store is Ladurée and as you probably already expect, this store originated in Paris. We will have to go inside. Liisi, a beautiful blond from Slovenia, welcomes us. No matter how charming the hostess is, we came here for the macaroons and find fifteen different kinds that change according to season. The most outstanding flavours are licorice, rose, and Diva. The last one contains grapefruit, spices and white chocolate. Don't miss this one; Liisi would love to see you.

We already mentioned the famous Harrods store, but we also visited Fortnum and Mason in Piccadilly. You can't miss it; it has the classic green façade and baroque elements. The history of this house goes back to 1707. Here, there are more English delicacies than Harrods. Every counter is in itself a candy store. We feel immediately at home between the tall jars of jelly and chewing gum. Behind the counter are boxes full of fudge. We also find a counter with a variety of pâtisserie houses; we see desserts from Sketch and wedding cakes from the Little Venice Cake Company, a tart shop, which we will visit later. We are thrilled to meet Sue, who sells muffins, scones and authentic English delicacies in her little shop. We are happy that we still find some form of tradition.

A totally different culture we find further down the street. Minamoto Kitchoan is a Japanese pâtisserie. The shop is straight and somber; the pâtisserie is intriguing and unknown to us. We get explanation from Yui, the sales lady, who is trying to do her best to speak English, which is not easy for her. Fortunately we get quite far with the body language of hand and feet. This little shop gets its delicacies imported from Japan, where they are produced in Okayama. Many creations are made from rice and beans. Tsuya is the favorite, which resembles two pancakes filled with sweet red beans. Another noticeable delicacy is sakuranbo, a candied cherry in jelly. The style of this Japanese pâtisserie is firm and without fuss.

176

# William Curley

This is one of the most well known pâtissiers of London, reachable
via the Metro to Richmond. This small village in the southwest of the
metropolitan city has an exuberance of its own. The history of this
village goes back to Henry I, who lived around 1299. It is here where the
Rolling Stones first performed. In one of the back alleys we find the small
pâtisserie shop of William Curley. Suzue, his wife, welcomes us warmly.
There is a small table where you can enjoy a cup of tea and a pastry.
The pâtissier comes originally from Scotland, born in the hamlet of Fefe,
which was a village of mostly blue-collar workers. William tells his story:
"I never wanted to become a pâtissier. To be honest, I was not good at
anything in school. My father was very strict and insisted that I learned a
trade, so I went to a trade school. There they taught you different things:
metalworking, woodcarving and cooking, which was attended mainly
by girls. I chose the last one and was the only boy between all the girls.
Maybe that was the reason I continued in this," he smiles. "There we
started with baking scones and pancakes. I liked it and assisted a pastry
chef, who always took care of the dessert trolley, which I loved. For me
no more fish or chicken. I'd rather have sticky hands." One thing led to
another and the chef decided to follow this passion with national and
international experiences. For example, William worked at the pâtisserie
of Pierre Romeyer, with Pierre Koffman at La Tante Claire and in Oxford
with Raymond Blanc. The last chefs have really inspired the very friendly
William. Then came Marco Pierre White. "That topped it all, because that
man was crazy! He didn't just think of food, but of everything and
everything had to be more than perfect. It was all about the total package
and that is something I learned from him. I didn't learn to make another
lemon soufflé, but more how to perfect the old one." When William was
28, he moved to the Savoy Hotel in London where he became the leader
of 21 pâtissiers. Here he learned to organize, to make showpieces and to
work in high volumes. At that time he also took part in different
competitions, one of them the Coupe du Monde in Lyon. That was the
time he decided to start his own business. It took him a year to find an
appropriate property. The centre of London was incredibly expensive, so
he chose Richmond, which now is one of the most thriving neighbor-
hoods of London. In the beginning it was difficult to educate the people
of this village what real pâtisserie was, as they were used to butter tarts

and shortbreads. But now this Scot has become one of them! His pâtisserie is fabulous, with small touches of Japan, the influence of his Japanese-born wife. In 2007, William was named the Best Chocolatier of London. Although this is a passion for him, he is not blinded by it. One of his dreams is to open a shop in Japan or Paris, even though he already owns three stores. "Yeah, a shop in Paris... that would be fun!" William is happy to share a recipe with us. "A recipe is not sacred, I didn't invent the egg!" Later, he has another surprise for us.

### Tuscan chocolate and orange bombe

*For 10 bombes:* 4 candied orange peels, chocolate gallettes, gold leaf.

*For the Tuscan mousse:* 450 g Tuscan chocolate 66%, 90 g sugar, 45 g water, 150 g egg yolk, 570 g loosely whipped cream.

*For the Grand Marnier crème:* 500 g milk, 1 vanilla bean, 60 g egg yolk, 110 g sugar, 50 g flour, 4 sheets of gelatin, 50 g white chocolate, 100 g Grand Marnier, 500 g fluffy whipped cream.

*For the caramelized orange:* 12 segmented oranges, 250 g sugar, 100 g orange juice.

*For the chocolate biscuit:* 400 g eggs, 100 g egg yolk, 200 g unsalted butter, 160 g sugar, 50 g flour, 50 g cornstarch, 60 g cocoa powder, pieces of hazelnuts.

*For the layer of chocolate praline:* 200 g milk chocolate, 150 g hazelnut praline paste, 180 g feuillantine, 20 g cocoa powder.

*For the glaze:* 1400 g water, 1800 g sugar, 600 g cocoa powder, 1000 g cream, 100 g gelatin.

For the mousse, melt the chocolate; whisk the egg yolks, heat water and sugar to 121ºC/250ºF. Prepare as pâté à bombe and let cool. Mix the cream with the pâté à bombe and carefully blend in the chocolate. For the cream, bring the milk and the vanilla bean to a boil. Mix the egg yolks with the sugar and flour and prepare as crème pâtisserie. Melt chocolate in the hot cream with Grand Marnier and blend together until smooth. With a spatula mix the cream with the crème pâtissier.

Caramelize the sugar and deglaze with the orange juice. Marinate this in the cooled cream mixture. For the biscuit, beat the eggs, egg yolks and the sugar au bain-marie. Sift the flour, cornstarch and cocoa powder. Carefully add pieces of butter to the sabayon and put in a mould. Mix in the flour and spread thinly on a silicon pat, sprinkle crushed hazelnuts on top. Bake the biscuit at 200ºC/390ºF for 18 minutes. Let cool and cut ring forms out of the biscuit and temper with diluted Grand Marnier. For the feuillantine, melt the chocolate and mix with the rest of the ingredients. Pour on baking sheet and let harden. For the glaze, heat the water and sugar for 2 minutes. Add the cocoa powder and cream and boil for another 5 minutes. Slightly cool, add the pre-soaked gelatin and strain through a fine-mesh sieve. Fill the bombe forms with the bitter chocolate mousse, cover with a thin layer of cream and a slice of chocolate praliné. Place the squeezed orange on top followed by the bitter chocolate mousse. Finish with a piece of biscuit, freeze the bombes, invert the forms on a plate and glaze.

**www.williamcurley.co.uk**

## Melt

During this trip, the Metro has become our best friend and so we stop in Notting Hill. Our editor realizes that he probably is the only one who has never seen the film with the same name. Melt is located at Ledbury Road 59. Here the key word is chocolate. The area is upper class, or as our host Keith Hurdman calls it: "The poor with a lot of money." The small shop was started by Louise Nason. She apparently is the wife of a super rich banker and this is her serious hobby. Because she loves to eat chocolate herself, she needed professional help. Fortunately we discover that we deal with passion and skill here, thanks to Keith Hurdman. This Englishman worked for several years in Switzerland, where he worked with chocolate but also taught classes. Back in London, he was approached by Louise. Truth be told, the shop is a delight for the eyes. Customers don't have to stand in front of the counter and gaze at the pralines, but can help themselves and take their sweet treats with wooden tongs. Freedom galore! At the end of the store is Keith's area, an open chocolate corner, where everyone can see how the delicacies are made. The chef works with a diverse group of people. Jin from Japan, and Giovanna and Lorenzo from Italy. Apprentices come from all over the world to be taught the art of chocolaterie. We ask Keith what his secret is. "We produce everything ourselves. Homemade here means homemade. We love to show the public. Some people can watch us for hours and bombard us with endless questions. The clients here get fresh pralines. What we make goes directly into the shop. People often buy bonbons to keep them in a box for weeks. Get rid of that keeping mentality. We don't keep a large supply or a steady assortment. Our flavours are seasonal." Although many chocolatiers stick with one brand, our chef looks at every brand and picks his favorite. His tasting palate is selective. He doesn't like strange flavours or silly stuff. "I like it when the customers want to eat their pralines right in the store. As I said I don't want freak shows. I like to work with spices, which come from the colonial past of England. Your pink magazine gave me a basic idea. However, I like to combine just a few flavours, like strawberries with bitter ganache of 71% or caramel with salt." Keith loves to talk, but unfortunately we have to move on. He gives us a nice tip. Just around the corner is Tea Palace, where they serve 156 kinds of tea. They are in beautiful tins and of course afternoon tea is also an option.

**www.meltchocolates.com**

## The Dessert Bar

This is the evening we have looked forward to. William had already promised to take us to the pâtisserie-hotspot in London. The Metro stopped at Green Park and via a side street of Piccadilly we turn into a small alley, called Shepherd Market. Here, William has his second shop, a dessert bar. This is a dream for every dessert lover, because it is here where Vicki instantly makes the most delicious desserts for her guests. You can sit at the bar equipped with bar stools and a dessert menu in front of you. What would you think of a baba with rum and caramelized pineapple, glazed with sautéed butter, or a millefeuille of chocolate made with hazelnut dacquoise with orange yogurt ice cream and yuzu jelly? This you can eat with a special cup of chocolate milk, made with a variety of spices or with chili powder. Of course, a cup of English tea or coffee is also possible. It is a great concept, which would certainly work in other countries as well. Why did William start this kind of business and not an ordinary shop? "A second shop was necessary, but I wanted more, something people would talk about. The dessert bar is a great success. In the summer we make beautiful ice cream creations. The best part is that people start asking questions about the desserts, which makes them interested in our profession."

## La Belle Epoque

Many pâtisseries in London are of French origin. The French, in contrast to the English, understand that a pâtisserie in a metropolitan city can be quite lucrative. Our Metro stops at Angel Station, after which we take bus line 73 to arrive at La Belle Epoque. Eric and Hülya Rousseau are the proud owners, a marriage between a Turkish woman and a French man. The name of the shop relates to art nouveau, which was for Eric the time that everything was made by hand and skilled labour was sublime as evidenced by Tiffany and the Fabergé eggs. The business is a bit of France in England or as Eric says: "English pieces with a French twist." Our chef learned the trade in many countries. Besides France, he also worked in hotels in Namibia, South Africa and Guatemala.

Eventually he ended up in London with Jean Christophe Novelli. He was involved in receiving a Michelin star, but also with the bankruptcy. He realized that owning your own business needs a good foundation. In the little shop, they sell pâtisserie as well as bread, of course all in French tradition. They are very proud of their La Belle Epoque tart, made with Cuban chocolate and a creamy orange crème brûlée with Grand Marnier and feuilletine. After tasting this, we couldn't agree more with the chef.

www.belleepoque.co.uk

## Paul A Young

We stay around Angel Station, as it is only a one-minute walk to our next address. Paul A Young has been recommended to us by many of our pâtissier colleagues. In a very short time, this 34-year-old has built a great reputation on chocolate. We find his first shop in the neighbourhood of Islington, a prosperous suburb of London. Paul was born in Yorkshire and grew up in Durham in northeast England. According to the chef, it is an area where it is often dark, somber and cold. After a few kitchen jobs, he was discovered by one of the chefs of Marco Pierre White, who was then at the top of his popularity in catering. Refusal was no option, as he would never get a second chance. Paul: "I worked six years with Marco, which is a long time. Most people didn't stay that long. Coincidentally, I was hired just as William Curley was leaving. After this experience, I continued in pâtisserie. I did some free-lance for television and some magazines. After that I worked a year for Marks & Spencer

and at Sainsbury's, where I learned the business side of things, the way I should be marketing and that kind of stuff. Making pâtisserie is one thing, but selling is another. After developing new ideas for these stores, I started to realize that other people became successful with my stuff. That made me start my own business." With its strong aubergine colours, this little shop is sweet and cozy. Less sweet are the prices of real estate. According to Paul, this is the reason why many young people cannot start their own business. Paul: "Just think that we are not even in the centre of town, but in a suburb. For a shop like mine, you would have to pay 4000 pounds a month for rent." We see many certificates on his wall, prizes for Paul's creations. The chef has a variety of chocolate delicacies with an average of twenty-four pralines. Next to the classic flavours, there are also special ones, like Pimm's truffles. Pimm's is an alcoholic beverage you normally drink with cucumber, mint and strawberries. In 2007 Paul made this cocktail into a bonbon. What would you think of whiskey bonbons or a ginger saffron bonbon? Among the classic flavours is a prizewinner that is the caramel praline with sea salt, which has been acclaimed as the best praline of England. In his workshop, the chef doesn't have a tempering machine. Everything is done by hand. "We don't want to work with machines, because our customers don't like to see identical bonbons. We just temper on a marble slab and I think it gives the best result." Beside the shop in the Camden Passage, Paul also has a

job at Threadneedle Street. Next year, he will open a shop in New York City, and we think this is just a beginning. Paul is happy to share some of his secrets with you.

www.paulayoung.co.uk

### Saffron and honey praline

*For about 250 pralines:* 1000g Valrhona Ivoire couverture, 600 ml mineral water, *1 tsp saffron, 400 g honey, milk chocolate.*

Bring the water to a boil, add the saffron and honey and let simmer for 5 minutes. Then bring to a boil again, take off the burner and add the chocolate. Blend together to get a smooth mixture. Cool the ganache, line forms with tempered milk chocolate and let harden. Fill the forms with the ganache and finish the pralines. Garnish with the Ivoire chocolate.

### Pimm's Cocktail truffles

*For about 250 truffles:* 1 bottle of Pimm's, 200 g cleaned organic cucumber, 150 g blackberries, 25 g mint leaves, 350 ml mineral water, 200 g muscovado sugar, 1 kg Valrhona Nyangbo couverture, truffle balls of 68%, bitter couverture of 68%.

Press the cucumber through a juicer and repeat that three times with the cucumber liquid. Bring the water and mint to a boil and cook for 3 minutes. Chop the mint leaves with a hand blender and cool in the liquid. Drain the liquid and bring to a boil with the sugar. Add the Pimm's, heat slightly, dissolve the chocolate and blend until smooth. Let cool and fill the truffle balls. Dredge them in 68% bitter couverture.

### English Rose Truffle

*For about 250 truffles:* 1 kg Caraibe couverture 66%, 700 ml mineral water, 30 drops of English rose oil, 450 g sugar, truffle balls of 55%, bitter couverture of 66%.

Bring water, sugar and cream to a boil, let cool slightly and fold in the chocolate until smooth. Add the oil and mix well so the oil will dissolve. Let cool and fill the truffle balls. Pull through 66% bitter couverture.

P09

# Haute Couture

A visit to England without getting a glimpse of the wedding cake tradition would be close to impossible. Our Metro stops at Bakerstreet Station, from where we have to walk 10 minutes to Manchester Mews, a small alley in the suburb of Marylebone. Here you will find the Valhalla of all the wedding cakes in London. Mich Turner started her shop in 1999 in the district of Little Venice, hence the name of Little Venice Cake Company. The business grew and had to move to Manchester Mews. Besides the business her reputation also grew, because she made cakes for the stars, like Madonna, Pierce Brosnan and Sir Paul McCartney. Even Queen Elizabeth feasted on her cake when she had her 60th Jubilee. We meet Camilla, who has worked with Mich for years; she tells us how it all works: "When customers come in for a cake, it can be for any occasion. We start with a consultation and together we create the ideal cake. We have different folders that show previously made tarts. While our customers browse through the folders and choose their favorite cakes, I go downstairs to the kitchen to bring them suggestions for flavours. We have five flavours, three are basic butter crème, a carrot cake and a rich fruit cake. The last one is similar to a Christmas pudding and is traditionally sold the most." Choosing a cake one has to think of the preferred taste of each guest. England has a tradition where one keeps the top piece of each cake, which can be eaten at the baptism of the first child or the first wedding anniversary. For this the carrot cake and fruitcake are the most suitable. After the right flavour and style are chosen, one looks at the colour the cake should have. One also looks at the theme colours in combination for the big day. Once the cake has been decided, they can start the process.

The bakery of the cake shop, where twenty bakers are employed, is a bit outside the city. The cakes then go the decoration workshop, where we find Cristine and Anneri. Cristine specializes in the garnish of fondant. It started as a hobby, but by studying books, practice and experience, she is now a master. Anneri was born in South Africa and specializes in moulding and working with chocolate. The cake is first covered with a layer of marzipan. With so-called smoothers this layer is firmly pressed on top and around the cake. On top of this layer comes a layer of rolled fondant. Once this layer has dried, the finishing can start. There are several ways to make small patterns. The simplest are small dots, but simple? No pointed parts are allowed. Next is pressure piping, a small dot

of piped glazing, which will be twisted in a desired shape, and is ideal for the classic Victorian symbols. They also decorate with straight lines, but this technique is more difficult than you think. We speak from experience, as the editor tried his version of it. The patterns are placed on the cake with stencil paper. Small marks are made on the stencil paper with a sharp pin to indicate where the ladies must stop piping. If you are interested in specializing in the making of wedding cakes, you can order the spectacular book Spectacular Cakes available at the website of Little Venice Cake Company.

We are curious if there are also trends in cakes. Anneri: "Nowadays, you see cakes change just like fashion, particularly in patterns and colours.

It used to be all classic and in baroque style. Today, cakes can be very sober with just two colours or the opposite, rich in colours using very fresh tones. When it comes to flavours, everything is still rather classic." The orders come in full force when spring is here and the high season starts. We assume that Cristine can only work in a serene and quiet environment, as her work is of extreme precision. "I notice that if the pressure is off, my work improves. However, this business is rarely quiet; with some music in the background and work galore, I still like what I do."

**www.lvcc.co.uk**

## The Fat Duck

It takes about one and a half hours to travel between London and Berkshire. In the last few years The Fat Duck has become the Mecca of culinary aficionados and many chefs. It had been declared the best restaurant in the world! At the helm is Heston Blumenthal with a total crew of sixty people. Amongst the thirty-five chefs is Jocky, the chef-pâtissier. This time the attention is not on the famous chef. Jocky was born as James Petrir in the little Scottish village of Oban, known for its whiskey. The young guy grew up to be a chef and his nickname became Jocky, something he didn't like at first. When he started to work in a kitchen where five chefs were called James, he accepted his nickname. He had no intention to go into pâtisserie. "I always seemed to work in a restaurant or hotel that did not have a pâtissier in the kitchen. So I took that task. I liked it because I had my own little shop, which I had to manage every night. Many times I wanted to go back to the kitchen, but it never happened." After experiences in several top restaurants he wanted to work at The Fat Duck and it became possible as a sous-chef in the pâtisserie. Jocky smiles: "I didn't want to miss this opportunity; I thought it would be for a short time, but I have been there already for six years. Our kitchen is so small that everyone is involved. It is not that the pâtissiers only do desserts; the whole menu involves components that come from the pâtisserie."

The Fat Duck is known for its modern kitchen, but according to Jocky that should not be so. "We are currently specializing in the historical British kitchen. Many dishes and ingredients have been lost. Take for instance, the Black Forest cake, a classic cake, which we still like to honor. Of course, we like to make every dish perfect and we really research how to do that best. Another example is the classic Chantecler Apple dessert. Here we use malic acid, which is the acid of apples. This way we keep the flavours together. We are often at laboratories. Deliberately, we choose a location in a different building, where we can test and try things out in a quiet environment. Most important are the discussions and the freedom to express yourself. This brings us together. It takes about six months to develop a dish. Sooner or later you become engrossed in the process. I love my job and work eighteen hours a day, which gives me some extra money to go out for dinner. You should be able to taste the passion of your work on your plate."

Trying to be perfect is the slogan of the restaurant. Besides all the new ideas, it should also be delicious. "We play with flavours and try every-thing. At the moment we are looking for umami (the fifth taste). We look what is fresh in season, and it is not the gimmick but the flavour that counts. We always finish the menu with "The Sweet Shop", which are caramel toffees and violets. You can eat the foil as well, but it is made with methyl." In the lab we witness different experiments. Jocky is kind enough to make some dishes for us. Unfortunately the measurements of the ingredients will still be kept secret for the next book and we respect that. So we will have to wait until the next Fat Duck Cookbook, a compilation of all the recipes. Chef Blumenthal, who at the end of our visit shook hands with us, allowed us to publish a few of the recipes.

www.fatduck.co.uk

### *Black Forest Gateau*

*For the chocolate cake:* biscuit made of amarena cherries, white and dark chocolate mousse, amarena cherries, praline, fine almond nougatine.
*For the brittle:* milk chocolate, cocoa butter.
*For the kirsch ganache:* cream, kirsch, dark chocolate.
*For the cherries:* amarena cherries, a used vanilla bean pod.
*For the almond-cherry sauce:* almonds, cherry purée, amarena syrup.
*For the kirsch ice cream:* milk, non-fat milk powder, egg yolks, kirsch, sugar.

This cake consists of different layers. For the brittle, mix some tempered milk chocolate with some cocoa butter, pour in a siphon and insert two charges. Squirt in shapes and sous vide (vacuum cook) at 2 millibars (pressure that is used in the machine) in a temperature of 20°C/68°F. Let harden for one and half hours, freeze and cut with a serrated knife. Create a kirsch ganache with cream, kirsch and chocolate. The ganache should harden over three days. Make a traditional biscuit with amarena cherries and cover first with white and then with dark chocolate mousse. On the bottom of the cake is a layer of praline with fine almond nougatine. The cake is built in layers and finished with a velvety chocolate. Putting a lollipop stick in the middle will help with transportation, preventing it from falling apart. To serve this, remove the stick and fill the opening with amarena syrup. On the cake, put an amarena cherry and the stem of a vanilla bean. To create a stem for the cherry, cut half a vanilla pod in thin small strips, create a knot and put in a dehydrator to dry. To serve, cut the top off the knot and push it in the cherry. Garnish the cake with fleur de sel, colored with gold powder. For the sauce, blanch the almonds, peel and let hydrate in the water. Heat black cherry purée with amarena syrup and add the almonds. Blend the mixture, using a hand blender, until smooth. Heat the sauce, which should bind lightly. For the kirsch ice cream, make a classic anglaise with only milk, milk powder, kirsch and a few egg yolks. The composition will be pasteurized sous vide for 10 minutes at 70°C/158°F. Spin the ice cream after it has cooled. Garnish with a small chocolate galette and curls of chocolate, on which the ice cream is served.

D09

## Chantecler Apple

*For 4 people:* cream cheese, lightly sweetened, apple brunoise.
*For the small sheets of dough:* puff pastry, sugar, butter.
*For the apple filling:* Chantecler apples, sugar, butter, apple juice.
*For the paté de fruit:* some reserved apple syrup, malic acid, pectin.
*For the vanilla ice cream:* milk, non-fat milk powder, vanilla, egg yolks, sugar.
*For the liquid gel:* freeze-dried apples, water, malic acid, bay leaf, gellan.
*For the apple caramel milk:* whole milk, reserved apple peels and cores.
*For the apple chips:* very thinly sliced apples, sugar water 1:1, lime juice, salt.
*For the crumble:* unsweetened praliné, vanilla salt, brown butter, freeze-dried apple.

Roll out puff pastry dough very thin, coat with a small layer of butter and sprinkle with sugar. Bake dough between two silpats until crunchy. For the filling, core and peel the apples, save peels and cores for the apple caramel milk. Caramelize the sugar, add apples and butter. Deglaze with apple juice, let cool and keep syrup separately. Slice apples in thin slices and stagger on a baking sheet, cover with aluminium foil and keep in the fridge overnight. Press the mixture down to release the liquid. Cover with two sheets of aluminium foil and put in the oven au bain marie for seven hours at 100°C/210°F. Next, let set sous vide and cut to size. Make a paté de fruit with the reserved apple syrup, malic acid and pectin. After it has cooled, cut to size. For the vanilla ice cream, make a classic anglaise with milk, milk powder, vanilla and a few egg yolks. Pasteurize under vacuum for about 10 minutes at 70°C/158°F, Cool and spin the ice cream. For the gel, mix all the ingredients, heat to 85°C/185°F and remove bay leaf. Cool and mix to a smooth gel. Cook the apple caramel with the milk and rest of ingredients. If the mixture separates, stir and heat to 72°C/160°F. The mixture will clarify by itself. Pour through a cheesecloth. This liquid will be transparent. For the crumble, mix the ingredients, cool and chop. Build the millefeuille with the paté de fruit, the apple filling, the cream cheese with some apple brunoise and in between the puff pastry. Spread some crumble and gel on top and serve with ice cream and an apple chip. Draw an apple caramel line between the two.

## The sorbet

This dessert is still at an experimental stage and will probably change. It re-creates the feeling that Heston Blumenthal had when he had a campfire at his uncle's. Ice cream is used that doesn't melt! The elements give a crackling fire and the smell of warm leather.

*For four people:* 4 small pots, dry ice, crackling sugar, whiskey, apple brunoise, 4 deep soup plates with leather rim, 4 small wooden wreaths.
*For the sorbet:* freeze-dried apples, water, malic acid, bay leaf, gellan gum.

For the ice cream, mix the ingredients, heat to 85°C/185°F and remove bay leaf. Once cooled, mix to a smooth gel. Put the mixture in a Frix beaker, freeze and spin quickly. Heat the little pots in the oven at 200°C/390°F. Fill the plates with some dry ice and crackling sugar. Place the small wreath on top with the little pot in the center. Fill the little pot with pieces of apple and a quenelle of apple sorbet. Pour a bit of hot water under the little pot. The plate will start to smoke and sizzle. Pour a bit of whiskey in the pot and flambé the ice. This gives you the sensation of a crackling campfire.

# Marike van Beurden

*A Dutch gal amongst the Parisians*

You know it has to be a great story when a young Dutch girl throws herself between male French chefs involved in their country's haute cuisine. 25-year-old Marike van Beurden took on this tough task at the Michelin 3 star restaurant Le Cinq in the Paris hotel George V. We are very proud of her.

Marike's restaurant is in a hotel that really shows what luxury and grandeur means. We first got to know her when she participated in the Dutch Pastry Awards. At that time she was working in London at Sketch, run by Pierre Gagnaire. She is just 165 cm (5ft. 5inches) tall, in contrast to her ambitions. But she did win the Dutch Pastry Award, which gave her the opportunity to be part of the Dutch National Pastry Team. Marike was honored and welcomed the opportunity to grow in her profession. A few years later she left London for a bustling Paris. Marike walks towards us as we were having a cup of tea in the magnificent breakfast lounge. The mostly American tourists keep eyeing her, her very walk tells you she is full of confidence in her job. Marike confesses she slept only three hours last night as she stayed up late preparing for our meeting. What more can we say? After three years of working in

Paris, how did she find her niche? "When I arrived here I did not speak one word of French. It was difficult, very difficult. Instead of Marike, I am called Gouda. The French attitude toward foreigners can discourage many and I can very well understand that. Fortunately there are more foreigners working here, but even so, it's not easy. That is behind me now and I can cope with it. The reason why I work in France is because it is great for my career." Marike suggests giving us a tour, so off we go...

## Competition

Our pâtissière is busy with many competitions and dedicates a lot of her time to that, but her dedication has paid off. Last August she won the prestigious Trophée Carol Duval-Leroy. We wonder how she can combine her work and competitions. "Competitions are very important

to me and I try to do as many as possible. You expand your horizons and you force yourself to try new things. I do my practices mostly at night, as I don't have any time during the day. I do all competitions in my own time." She continues, smiling. "Sometimes it happens that I skip a night's sleep. Many colleagues call me crazy; they tell me that I have no life. Are they right? I don't think so. Because I like my life as it is. Those people have a different mentality, they work and then they go home." Maybe we have to call Marike a workaholic. One would think that the prizes this young girl earns would demand a lot of respect from her colleagues. "Respect? Maybe, but also a lot of envy and jealousy. Sometimes it is difficult for my French colleagues to see a Dutch person winning. It has happened more than once that my showpieces, which I have made at night, are broken the next day! Mysteriously nobody seems to know anything about it. But the management, like the maître, the director and the chef, they do give me that respect. That makes me proud." While Marike gives us the tour, she is telling us that she does have good relations with some of the employees. They made extra space for her in the wine cellar for her showpieces. Marike takes us to that cellar. Our hearts pound when we see the amazing selection of wines. "It is a must for me to have good relations with the sommeliers, sometimes I participate in wine/spice competitions. Who can give me better advice?" By accident we bump into a bottle of Chateau d'Yquem, nearly breaking it and realize that the price of this one bottle is the value of a nice vacation. We put the bottle back carefully and quickly move on. Is Marike ready for a world competition? "All these competitions are a preparation for that. Let me tell you that I want to be well prepared for the competi-

tion in Lyon, the Coupe du Monde." That Marike takes this seriously is clear to us. But what about a place on the Dutch National Team? Is that no option? "It would be a great honour, but it is impossible for me to do all the traveling while I am practicing. Maybe become part of the French team, although that may be impossible. Or maybe I will just marry a French man and will try to become a French Master Chef," she jokes. Or is that no joke?

## Sometimes I act like a bitch

The tour continues and her Pastry in Europe chef's jacket draws a lot of attention from her colleagues. "I think I will hear about this for a long time". After just a few hours we hear her colleagues calling her Pink Panther and Barbie and these are just a few of the names. How does she cope with being of the 'wrong' nationality and being a woman in a man's world? "We have quite a few women in the kitchen, except that they tolerate men more than women. In the meantime my colleagues have discovered that they cannot fool around with me. I am getting more responsibilities. Our pastry department has fourteen people and besides the desserts for the restaurant, we also make pastries for the rest of the hotel. If my chefs are not available, I have to take all responsibility. Just remember that a dessert, except soufflés, have to be on the table within 15 minutes. Then sometimes I become a bitch, but it has to be good, no exception." Strong language, but we like it. She continues: "Don't get scared, because it is a great place to work, where people take good care of you and most of my colleagues are sweethearts." In the meantime we have arrived at the pastry kitchen, where Marike prepares for making the desserts for our report. One of her colleagues immediately makes room for her; a subtle hint to move is enough. Our pâtissière names one source of inspiration, a winner of the Coupe du Monde: Christof Michalak. His working style is similar to Marike's and it is her wish to work together one day. We can describe that style as "daring", but we also admire her ambition to reach to these heights.

### Fig tart with Passito di Pantelleria

**For the bottom of the pastry tart:** 300 g flour, 200 g butter, 100 g white granulated sugar, 1 egg, 1 vanilla bean, 2 g lemon zest.
**For the almond filling:** 8 eggs, 500 g butter, 500 g sugar, 500 g almond powder, 20 g dark rum, 1 tsp cinnamon.
**For the fig compôte:** 1 tsp butter, 2 lime peels, 1½ cinnamon stick, 200 g Passito di Pantelleria, 1 tbs sugar, fresh figs.
**For the jelly:** 225 g Passito di Pantelleria, 75 g water, 2 sheets of gelatin.

Use a mixer with a dough hook and mix all the ingredients for the bottom of the tart. Create a supple dough and cool in the fridge. For the almond filling whisk the eggs with the butter and add the rest of the ingredients. For the compote, peel the figs, cut in slices and cook with the other ingredients. For the jelly, mix the ingredients (except the gelatin) and bring to a boil, let cool and put the soaked gelatin in it. Roll out the pastry dough, grease the bottom of the pastry pan, cover the bottom with the dough, fill with a small layer of almond filling and bake in the oven at 175ºC/350ºF until golden brown. Take out of the oven and fill with the compôte, cover with a layer of fig slices and finish with the jelly.

### Granita made of pineapple and hibiscus with tropical fruit and coconut with lychee cream

**For lychee cream:** 200 g lychee purée, 40 g milk, 48 g egg yolks, 50 g sugar, 20 g milk powder, 40g flour, whipping cream.
**For the coconut foam:** 100 ml cream, 100 ml milk, 25 g sugar syrup (1:1), 100 ml coconut purée, 10 g pasteurized egg white, 10 g water.
**For pineapple compote:** 300 g pineapple, 140 g mashed bananas, 250 g passion fruit coulis, 100 g mango coulis, 300 g water, 100 g sugar.
**For hibiscus granité:** 1 kg hibiscus basis, 1 kg pineapple purée, 700 g water.
**For the pineapple-coconut sorbet:** 1200 g fresh pineapple purée, 750 g coconut purée, 380 g water, 420 g sugar, 160 g glucose, 12 g stabilizer.
**For the coconut tuile:** 400 g sugar syrup (1:1), 40 g honey, 100 g grated coconut.

For the cream, boil the milk with the lychee purée. Mix the egg yolks with the sugar, milk powder and flour and pour the hot cream on top of the yolk mixture. Mix well and pour back in the pan; let boil for another few minutes and cool. Per 140 g cream, blend in 80 g whipped cream. For the foam, mix all ingredients and whisk fluffy with a handheld blender. Cut pineapple in small cubes, bring the rest of the ingredients to a boil and let the pineapple cook until soft and well done. For the granité, mix the ingredients and create a granité. For the sorbet, boil the water, glucose and sugar, add the rest of the ingredients, cool and blend at high speed (turbine). For the tuile, mix the ingredients, smooth out on a silpat and bake at 175ºC/350ºF. To build this dessert, put a small layer of cream on the bottom, pour compote on it, and divide the foam around it. Finish with the granité and garnish with the tuiles.

### Exotic dessert shooter

**For the mango jelly:** 500 ml mango purée, 150 g water, 3 sheets of gelatin.
**For the coconut panna cotta:** 500 ml cream, 220 g coconut purée, 90 g raw sugar, 2½ sheets of gelatin.
**For the compôte of exotic fruit:** 100 g mango, 100 g kiwi,

100 g papaya, 100 g pineapple, 80 g water, 20 g sugar, 8 g lemon juice, 4 g pectin, 500 g passion fruit purée.
*For exotic foam:* 100 g papaya purée, 100 g guave purée, 100 g passion fruit purée, 15 g sugar syrup (1:1), 40 g pasteurized egg white.

For the jelly, mix the mango purée with the water and dissolve the soaked gelatin in it. For the panna cotta, heat the cream, coconut purée and the sugar and dissolve the soaked gelatin. For the compôte, clean the fruits and dice in small pieces. Boil the rest of the ingredients, cool and mix with the fruit. For the foam, mix all the ingredients, pour in a siphon and insert two chargers. Put the little shooter glasses on a slant in a small egg container, pour jelly in the glasses and let gel. Pour a little layer of compote on top and finish with the foam and a pineapple chip.

## Marike's Trophée dessert

**Delicious dessert of strawberry and crunchy tomatoes**

*For the tomato crumble:* 200 g almond powder, 200 g sugar, 200 g flour, 160 g butter, 60 g tomato purée, 2 g salt, 1 drop of red colouring.
*For the strawberry and tomato compôte:* 100 g brunoise of tomato flesh, 100 g brunoise of strawberries, 20 g strawberry purée, 25 g clear jelly.
*For the yogurt ice -cream:* 500 g yogurt, 25 g sugar, 50 g whole milk, 2 g stabilizer, 20 g lemon juice, 5 g trimoline.
*For the strawberry tuile:* 150 g 60% cooked strawberries, 70 g butter, 100 g icing sugar, 100 g flour, 80 g egg white.
*For the rhubarb foam:* 150 g rhubarb water, 20 g sugar syrup

(1:1), 100 g cream, 2½ sheets of gelatin.
*For the strawberry juice:* 125 g water, 500 g strawberry juice, 125 g raspberry purée, 80 g Samba mix (mix of different kind of flowers and fruit, including hibiscus).
*For the rhubarb granité:* 50 g rhubarb water, 100 g strawberry juice, 100 g Champagne Duval-Leroy Lady rose, 15 g sugar syrup.
*For the sugar-star:* 450 g fondant, 180 g glucose, 1 tsp dried red fruit powder.
*For the rhubarb and strawberry coulis:* 50 g rhubarb water, 50 g strawberry juice, 20 g sugar syrup (1:1), 8 g pectin.

For the crumble, mix all ingredients, roll out on a baking sheet and bake at 160ºC/320ºF in a convection oven. Cut the crumble in sharp triangles. Cook the compôte with the fruit and purée, add the jelly and cook for another 1 or 2 minutes. Cool on a platter and repeat making triangles that are the same as the crumble. For the yogurt ice cream, cook the sugar, milk, stabilizer and trimoline, let cool and mix with the yogurt and the lemon juice. Mix at high speed, smooth out on a platter, cool in the freezer and slice the same size triangles. Immediately stack the different triangles on top of each other for serving. For the tuile dough, mix all ingredients, smooth out on a silpat and bake at 180ºC/356ºF for 9 minutes. Wrap around a small tube. For the foam, heat the rhubarb water with the sugar syrup, dissolve the soaked gelatin in it, pour in the cream and stir well. Pour in a siphon and insert a charger. Pipe the foam directly in the tuile. For the strawberry juice, cook the water with the juice and purée, add the Samba mix and let reduce for about 20 minutes. For the granité mix the ingredients and create a granité. For the sugar-star, boil the fondant and the glucose to 160ºC/320ºF, let harden and grind to a powder. Mix this powder with the fruit powder and pour through a sieve on a silpat. Pre-heat oven to 200ºC/390ºF. Switch oven off and put the silpat in it. Take out of the oven when the sugar looks totally clear. Heat all ingredients for the coulis and add the pectin. Fill the sugar-star with the granité. Garnish the filled tuile with fresh raspberries and serve with the pastry triangle and coulis.

## Mango carpaccio with cranberry

*For the cookie of orange and chocolate:* 50 g butter, 180 g sugar, 50 g water, 75 g flour, 10 g cocoa powder, 50 g almond powder, 1 g salt, 3 orange-zests.
*For the cranberry and chocolate biscuit:* 10 g dark chocolate, 37 g butter, 37 g egg yolk, 30 g cranberry purée, 630 g egg white, 50 g sugar, 50 g flour.
*For the mango and cranberry ganache:* 120 g cranberry purée (without sugar), 120 g mango purée, 260 g white chocolate,

½ peel of a lime, 125 g whipping cream.
*For the cranberry compôte:* 200 g cranberry, 75 g water.
*For the mango brunoise:* 300 g mango brunoise, 600 g blood
orange juice.
*For the mango and orange sorbet:* 200 g mango purée (without
sugar), 800 g blood orange juice, 80 g sugar, 100 g glucose
powder, 220 g water, 8 g stabilizer, 20 g lemon juice.
*For the chocolate mousse:* 140 g dark chocolate, 60 g papua
chocolate, 450 g whipped cream, 350 g blood orange juice,
4 sheets of gelatin, 3 orange peels.
*For the fruit compôte:* 40 g cranberry purée (without sugar),
90 g fresh mango purée (without sugar), 15 g blood orange
juice with 10% sugar.
*For the cranberry and blood orange juice:* 200 g blood orange
juice with 10% sugar, 100 g cranberry purée (without sugar).
*For the mango carpaccio:* 1 mango.

For the cookie, finely chop the zests with the sugar, mix with the butter
and salt; add the rest of the ingredients and mix to a smooth consistency.
Create strips with the aid of a stencil of 3 x 16 cm. Bake the strips in the
oven at 190ºC/375ºF for 3 minutes and wrap around a small tube. For the
biscuit, melt the butter and the chocolate and whisk the egg whites with
the sugar till stiff. Mix chocolate, egg yolks and cranberry compôte to a
smooth ganache and combine it with the egg whites and flour using a
spatula. Pour part of this dough on a baking sheet (about 1 cm thick) and
bake in the oven at 190ºC/375ºF for 5 minutes. Roll out the other part of
the dough between 2 sheets of wax paper to make a very thin layer and
bake at 190ºC/375ºF for 4 minutes. Cut the biscuit as shown on the
picture, mold it and put aside. For the fruit ganache heat both purées,
dissolve the chocolate in it and add the chopped lemon peel.
Cool mixture, add the whipped cream and fill the rolled cookie with this
ganache. For the cranberry purée, cook the berries with water, mix to a
purée and put through a fine mesh sieve. For the compôte, bring sugar
and water to a boil, add the cranberries, cook for another 10 minutes and
set aside to cool.  Heat the blood orange juice and put in the mango to
marinate for 2 minutes. For the sorbet, cook the blood orange juice with
the orange peels and let stand for 15 minutes. Pass through a fine-mesh
sieve; add the glucose, water and mango purée. When it reaches
50ºC/120ºF, add the sugar and stabilizer, heat up again, add the lemon
juice, set aside to cool and mix at very high speed (turbine). For the
coulis, mix the requested ingredients, the same for the juice. For the
carpaccio, peel the mango and slice extremely thin on a slicer. Create a
little tart of the biscuit and the cranberry purée and wrap this in the fruit
brunoise. Pipe the ganache in the rolled cookie; serve with the chocolate
mousse, the sorbet and the mango carpaccio.

# Thierry Marx
## Château Cordeillan-Bages

It is like a dream to be a chef in a castle and that is the situation at Château Cordeillan-Bages. Close to Bordeaux, in the Médoc, this restaurant has deserved its recognition more than once and according to the little red bible, is worth making a detour. Rumours have it that the third Michelin star will be received very soon. The philosophy of this chef is unique and obvious in his dishes: removing disturbing aspects in a product and replacing them by building in new components. Nothing is left to chance at Thierry's; everything has been thoroughly planned and thought through. He leaves the finishing to his support and assistants, Mickael Tanguy and Jean-Luc Rochas.

**www.cordeillanbages.com**

## Licorice root and red beet

*For 4 people:* 4 strings of licorice.
*For the licorice root ice cream:* 250 g milk, 180 g icing sugar,
33 g fructose, 90 g cream, 25 g milk powder, 6 g licorice
root powder.
*For the licorice root spiral:* 75 g muscovado sugar, 225 g water,
1.25 g agar-agar, 1 g licorice root powder.
*For the preserved red beet:* 500 g red beet, 250 g icing sugar,
250 g orange juice, ½ star anise, ¼ cinnamon stick.

Use cornet forms and heat them for one minute in the oven at
180ºC/355ºF. Roll the licorice strings around them and cool. For the
ice cream, mix the ingredients and let rest in a Frix Air beaker for
12 hours. Put beakers in the freezer and mix at very high speed when
frozen. Fill the cornets with ice cream and freeze. For the spiral, heat
the water, sugar, and licorice root powder, add the agar-agar and push
through a sieve. Squeeze the liquid in a small and thin tube, take the jelly
out of the tube and form into a spiral. For the preserved red beet, cut the
cleaned beets in brunoise, and cook slowly in the orange juice with sugar,
star anise and the cinnamon. Vacuum bag the beets and the liquid and
heat for 45 minutes in water bath of 65ºC/150ºF.

## Strawberry soup with turnip and glazed cannelloni

*For 4 people:* 1 long turnip, 200 g strawberries, olive oil.
*For the strawberry soup:* 30 g water, 12 g sugar, 6 mint leaves,
200 g strawberries, juice of ½ a lemon.
*For the lime jelly:* 80 g lime juice, 25 g water, 25 g sugar,
4 g agar-agar, 2 sheets of gelatin.
*For the strawberry Campari ice cream:* 80 g strawberries,
40 g water, 20 g sugar, 1 tsp lemon juice, 2 g crème anglaise,
10 g Campari.
*For the cannelloni:* 150 g sugar, 2,5 g pectin, 100 g butter,
50 g glucose, 50 g water.

Slice the turnip in very thin slices and marinate in olive oil for 24 hours.
Cut strawberries in thin slices. Mix all ingredients for the soup, puree
with a hand held food processor and pour through a fine mesh sieve.
For the jelly, heat the limejuice with water and sugar, dissolve in it the
agar-agar and pre-soaked gelatin, pour on a plate and cool in the fridge.
For the ice cream, puree the strawberries with water and lemon juice,
pass through the sieve, add the Campari and mix with the crème
anglaise. Let cool in the fridge and process with an ice cream mixer.
For the cannelloni, mix all the ingredients, stir well, spread thinly on a
silpat and bake in the oven at 180ºC/355ºF until golden brown. While it
is still warm, cut straight rectangles and form into small rolls. Build a
little tower in the centre of a soup plate with a small layer of strawberries, jelly, and marinated turnip; fill the cannelloni with ice cream
and pour the soup in the plates at the dinner table.

## Apple tagliatelle

*For 4 people:* 2 apples.

*For the syrup:* 1 litre water, 500 g sugar, 3 g lemon juice, 2 g salt.

*For the cardamom sauce:* 250 g milk, 250 g cream, 100 g egg yolk, 80 g sugar, 20 g roasted cardamom pods.

*For the spice jelly:* 700 g water, 70 g sugar, 2 cinnamon sticks, 2 vanilla beans, 20 g fresh ginger, 4.8 g agar-agar, 2 sheets of gelatin.

*For the lime granité:* syrup 30°B, lemon juice.

Carve the apple into tagliatelle using an appropriate grater. For the syrup, mix all ingredients together and heat, reducing to a syrup. Pour over the apple tagliatelle and cool. For the sauce, cook the milk, cream and the cardamom and let simmer for one hour. Push through a sieve. Beat the egg yolk with the sugar and make an anglaise. For the jelly, cook the water, sugar, cinnamon, vanilla, ginger and reduce to half. Push through a fine mesh sieve; add the exact amount of agar-agar and the pre-soaked gelatin. Pour in a small container, let cool and cut in cubes. For the granité, mix syrup and lime juice to 18°B and prepare as a granité.

# Amsterdam sour candies

When we talk about confiserie in Holland, we cannot leave out 'zuurtjes' or sour candies. In Amsterdam, we found a very trendy shop where this candy is being made in a professional and trendy way.

It all started in Barcelona with owners Dominik Otto and Marieken van den Brink. They both had finished their studies and decided to take a year off to relax. For them that meant studying Spanish in the capital of Catalonia. While they were doing their language course, they met two Australian guys who were starting a candy shop. A friendship developed, and Marieken was often seen at their shop, Papabubble, making candies. Once back in Holland, their passion had grown in such a way that the two of them decided to continue the concept in Amsterdam. They got support from Australia and slowly but surely started to master the technique of refining sugar. Two and a half years later, we meet their colleagues now running the shop in Amsterdam, South African James Dawson, and the very cheerful Australian Isobel Harper.

### A child in a candyshop

The shop in Amsterdam is not very large, but your eyes are immediately drawn to the zuurtjes and lollipops. The very colourful sight literally makes you feel like you are a child in a candy shop. It is relief to see that there is a real confiserie in the basement of the shop, where the general public can see how lollipops and zuurtjes are being made. Although the recipe is simple, the technique of making these little candies is a lot more

complicated. At Papabubble they are dedicated to using as much natural flavoring as possible, and they prefer using essential oils whenever they can. It's no problem doing this with citrus fruits and herbs like rosemary, but it doesn't work for every flavour. Only artificial flavouring will work for strawberries. Other complicating factors include temperature and humidity. Holland has a very changeable climate, which has a lot of influence on sugar. When it rains, the sugar becomes sticky, if the temperature is too high the sugar doesn't cool off, and dry air makes the sugar dusty. However, in conquering the details, Papabubble shows that candies are for everyone and that hip and trendy go very well together with craftsmanship and natural ingredients. It doesn't matter if it is a zuurtje with your own name on it, or an extra-extra-large lollipop with a diameter of twenty centimeters...

## Basic recipe for zuurtjes and lollipops

*Ingredients:* 12 kg sugar, 3 liters water, 3 kg glucose, 8 ml flavoring per 1 kg material, food coloring of your choice, citric acid to taste

Bring water and sugar to a boil and add the glucose and flavoring, continue to boil to 156°C/312°F and pour on a slab. Add coloring and citric acid.

We follow Isobel after she has cooked the syrup and poured it on a thick iron table. It is an old toffee table that can be cooled with water flowing underneath it. An iron ledge prevents the syrup from overflowing. The surface of the table and the ledge are coated with beeswax to stop the

stickiness of the sugar. The citric acid is then added to make the zuurtjes more sour. Because zuurtjes have different colours, they mix the colouring on the table with a palette knife. If the candies are made with one colour only, the colouring is added right away in the pan. If the sugar is cooled off sufficiently, the pieces will be divided by using a big pair of scissors. We are fortunate today, because they are creating zuurtjes with letters in it; a present from a romantic guy for his girlfriend. He must really love her or he is apologizing for something, because at Papabubble the minimum order is 10 kilograms. Of course the benefit is that you will have even more of a girlfriend to love after she has eaten all those candies!

## Rolling and Pulling

The colors are divided and the center of the zuurtjes will consist of blue letters with a white background. For this background, the sugar will be pulled or glazed; with this kind of volume a big hook is used and the sugar spun around it. Slowly, a beautiful soft glaze is created and the spectacle can start. The letters we see in the zuurtjes are all just square flat pieces. First, the outline of the letters is created with blue colored sugar, which is then filled with white sugar. Isobel tells us that the letters look slightly digital because of the many straight pieces. The letter Q is the most difficult one, because of its round form and a straight line. James glues the little squares together with a damp sponge. Normally, something damp should never be used when working with sugar, but here it helps to get the sticky effect. It is obvious that James has to work

according to the textbook. Although they both have lots of experience, it can still happen that a letter turns out to be upside down or is in the wrong spot. If this is discovered too late, they have to start all over again. Slowly we see the names of the two lovebirds and in the center of the zuurtje a little heart. Isobel creates the outside with the rest of the colours. If the sugar is a bit too cold, it is heated in the microwave. The table they work on is heated from the bottom with a thermostat adjusted to 90°C/195°F. The surface is finished with leather to prevent the sugar from sticking. In the meantime, the letters have been rolled into the sugar, and it is starting to look more like a large tree trunk with a diameter of 25 cm than a zuurtje. As Isobel is kneading a handle for the trunk with her hands, she lifts the giant mass up and spins it around. Suddenly the tree trunk looks more like a designer vase. The pulling has started and lasts until the tree trunk is only 1 cm wide. A little stick is cut every 80 cm, after which James rolls them into a round shape. The big letters are now diminished to a few millimeters. Our math tells us that we have created 50 metres of sour sticks that have been made from the start of this enormous mass. The little sticks are rapidly cut in small pieces, which results in at least 4000 zuurtjes. A last inspection guarantees that only perfect zuurtjes will be wrapped. The same technique is shown to us with lollipops. For this, an array of colours is rolled together, cut, and pushed in a tight can, which results in a straight lollipop.

**www.papabubble.com**

# Marc Meurin

*The Candy Magician*

In North America children and candy have an inextricable link. Chocolate bars, suckers and bubble gum all hold an important place in growing up, and grown-ups are quick to indulge their sweet tooth in exotic confections while eating out, but they are usually adult type desserts. In Northern France chef Marc Meurin allows adults to get back to their childhood in his Château de Beaulieu, a two-star Michelin restaurant housed inside a castle. Every adult leaves the restaurant with a stick of candy floss in their hand or a lollipop in their mouth. It is actually a status symbol in the neighborhood to suck on one of his lollipops, because it shows that you can afford to eat at Château de Beaulieu.  For years now, the owner and his chef-confisier Philippe Getineau have made a great assortment of candy, which is

served on a little carriage by your table. The guests have an enormous choice of incredible sweet delicacies, including ice creams based on well-known candies, such as carambar (a chewy caramel bonbon). Chef Meurin was the first in the world to have the courage to play with candies from childhood experiences, with the idea of creating unexpected magical moments. A new chapter has been added to the Château de Beaulieu with the recent addition of the 24-year-old Pastry Chef Ludovic Soufflet. A peek into the pastry kitchen there now reveals chefs wearing thick gloves and safety glasses experimenting with liquid nitrogen, keeping the candy machine of Marc Meurin in full swing.

www.le-meurin.fr

### Peanut Florentine

*Ingredients:* 75 g peanut butter, 100 g soft butter, 125 g flour,
50 g grated parmesan cheese, 500 g sugar, 50 g glucose, pecans,
sunflower seeds, cocoa nibs, raisins, pistachio nuts.

Mix the peanut butter, the butter, the flour and the parmesan cheese with
a whisk, smooth out on a silpat and bake in the oven. Caramelize the
sugar, the glucose and 100 g water. Crumble the baked dough and pour
caramel on top. Let cool and grind in coffee grinder. Pour this ground
powder in rectangle shapes of 6 x 2 cm. Garnish with the different nuts,
cocoa nibs and raisins and bake in the oven at 170°C/340°F for
5 minutes.

### Parmesan cookies with beet and small capers

*Ingredients:* 200 g butter, 250 g flour, 2 egg yolks,
250 g parmesan cheese, mayonnaise, small red beets,
capers in salt, vinaigrette.

Combine flour, butter, egg yolks and parmesan cheese in an electric
mixer. Let rest for a short while then roll the dough out to 1 cm thickness.
Using a sharp knife, cut in rectangular shapes and bake in the oven at
170°C/340°F. Cook beets, peel and cut in slices of 5 cm thick. Put a little
mayonnaise on the cookie and garnish with a slice of beet. Sprinkle some
vinaigrette over it and top with a caper.

## Meringue of red grapefruit, orange and ginger syrup

*Ingredients:* 200 g butter, 200 g egg whites, 800 g sugar, 250 g icing sugar, 60 g glucose powder, 500 g room, 1 vanilla bean, 5 egg yolks, 7 sheets of gelatin, orange blossom water, 5 oranges, fresh ginger, 10 g corn flour, 700 g grapefruit juice, 2 grapefruits, 2 red grapefruits.

Butter the inside of some cookie rings, line with polypropylene (thick plastic) and put in the fridge to cool. Use a mixer to beat egg whites with 250 g sugar and slowly add the icing sugar, using a spatula. Fill the rings with this and let dry for 2 hours in the oven at 85°C/185°F. Mix grape-fruit juice with 200 g sugar and add the glucose with 35 g water. Pour in a PacoJet and put in the freezer. Heat the cream with the vanilla bean. Beat the egg yolks with 150 g sugar until white in colour, pour in the cream, add 150 g butter and 2.5 sheets of soaked gelatin and keep in the fridge. Bring 500 g water to a boil with some orange blossom water, add 125 g sugar and 4 sheets of soaked gelatin. Slice grapefruit in segments and marinate in the sugar water. Boil the juice of 5 oranges and 125 g sugar to make the orange juice, add some freshly grated ginger. Bind with 10 g corn flour and pour through a sieve. Put the meringue in the centre of a plate and fill with the vanilla-cream. Garnish with segments of grapefruit and finish with orange juice. Add a sugar-spin as decoration.

## *Pomme d'Amour*
### Candy Apple

*Ingredients: Apples (watch size), 500 g sugar, 20 g water, 50 glucose, 20 g trimoline (invert sugar) red coloring.*

Sort apples to your preferred size and keep at room temperature. Boil water and sugar together with the glucose and trimoline to a temperature of 120°C/250°F. Then add the red colouring. Prick apple on a little lollipop stick. Heat the syrup to 150°C/300°F and dip apple in it, making sure it is completely covered in the hot caramel. Remove and let cool, stick end down on a rack until the caramel hardens.

## *Congolais*

*Ingredients: 100 g grated coconut, 125 g sugar, 40 g flour, 100 g egg white.*

Combine all ingredients in an electric mixer fitted with a flat beater and let rest for 12 hours. Create half-balls on a silpat. Bake for 20 minutes at 110°C/230°F and put 2 halves together. Roll through finely grated coconut. The chef uses the colours yellow, white and pink. Of course you can use other colours as well.

## Three mousses

*For white chocolate mousse:* 200 g white chocolate,
200 g heavy cream.
*For the licorice mousse:* 200 g licorice root, 500 ml water, and
4.5 sheets of gelatin, 375 g heavy cream.
*For the virtual smoked tea-mousse:* 1 bag of smoked tea,
500 ml water, 200 g sugar, juice of 3 lemons, 4 sheets of gelatin,
2 chargers.

For the chocolate mousse, melt the chocolate in a bain marie and then carefully add the whipped cream. Put the mixture in a metal kitchen ring, only half full, and let set in the fridge. For the licorice mousse, melt the licorice root and mix to make a smooth paste. Heat again and dissolve the soaked gelatin in it. Let cool and add the whipped cream. Fill the rings leaving 5 mm from the top. For the virtual tea mousse, let the hot tea, water and sugar steep and put the soaked gelatin in it to dissolve. Pour through a sieve, put in a siphon and add 2 chargers.

www.steiereck.at

# *A Vienna Symphony*
## Steirereck im Stadtpark

A beautiful park in the centre of busy Vienna is the ideal place to relax. In the midst of all
this green surrounded by sculptures of famous composers is the restaurant "Steirereck im
Stadtpark". Chef Heinz Reitbauer has an authentic and lighthearted kitchen; so don't think
of heavy Austrian dishes and bombastic chocolate cakes. Chef pâtissier Walter Schulz has
been working there for over twenty years and learned the trade from Heinz's father.
He has a creative mind and likes to stay aware of the modern trends. He believes that
desserts should not be too heavy. Instead of using cream and chocolate he prefers to use
herbs, a new trend that he discovered in the Benelux. He would rather use the sweetness
from fruits than that obtained from sugar or creams. He also prefers to work with products
from the countryside of Austria.

## Marinated pineapple with Arabic spices and cream of pina colada

*For the cream:* 200 g coconut puree, 300 g pineapple puree, 500 g whipping cream, 150 g egg white, 50 g crystal sugar, 5 sheets of gelatin, 50 ml white rum.

*For the pineapple sorbet:* 250 g pineapple puree, 25 g glucose powder, 60 g crystal sugar, 60 g water

*For the coconut cake:* 30 g flour, 30 g icing sugar, 30 g soft butter, 1 Tbs shredded coconut.

*For the marinated pineapple:* 250 g water, 125 g sugar, 2 cloves, 1 star anise, 1 cinnamon stick, 5 coriander seeds, ½ a vanilla bean, 5 anise seeds, ½ lemon peel, juice of 1 lemon, ½ a ripe Honduras pineapple.

Dissolve the pre-soaked gelatin in hot rum. Mix the pureed pineapple and coconut puree with the rum and let stew for a few minutes. Beat egg whites with sugar, mix with the coconut mixture and carefully blend in the whipped cream. Put in the fridge. For the sorbet mix all ingredients and spin. Mix all ingredients for the coconut cake at room temperature, except the shredded coconut, and put in fridge for 30 minutes. Spread a thin layer of dough as a circle, sprinkle with shredded coconut and bake at 200°C/390°F until golden. Roll up immediately after baking to form a cylinder.

For the marinated pineapple mix all ingredients, bring to a boil and let simmer for 30 minutes. Turn heat off and cut the peeled pineapple in thin slices. Marinate pineapple in the bouillon and simmer for at least 30 minutes. Pour 2 tablespoons of the cream in a soup bowl and cover with a few slices of pineapple. Use a piping bag, squeeze sorbet in the coconut cake and put on the plate. Finish the plate with dried pineapple.

## Pattaya mango with lovage, sallow thorn and spiced chocolate

*For four people:* 3 pattaya mangos, 2 sprigs of lovage, 125 ml sugar syrup 1:1, 1 lime, 4 tsp sallow thorn syrup, 1 large crumbling potato, 50 g white chocolate, 1 egg, 5 g crystal sugar, 1 sheet of gelatin, 10 g cream, 20 g white chocolate, ras el hanout (Moroccan spice blend), maldon salt (sea salt).

Beat egg and sugar until white; dissolve gelatin in 2 teaspoons sallow thorn syrup. Melt 50 g chocolate; mix with the syrup, the egg mixture and slightly whipped cream. Refrigerate a minimum of two hours. Peel potato, wash thoroughly and squeeze out liquid in a juicer. Work fast to avoid discolouring. Reduce liquid stirring constantly to get a thick batter. Pour between two silpats and roll into a very thin layer. Bake at 180°C/355°F until golden and break in coarse pieces. Cut 4 big slices of mango (1 mm thick) and 30 cubes of 15mm x 15mm. Puree rest of the pulp with the sugar syrup and press through a mesh-sieve. For the marinade, chop lovage very fine and mix with 2 tbs. mango puree and 2 tbs. sugar syrup. Add lemon juice to taste. Marinate the mango cubes in the liquid. For the spiced chocolate, cut the white chocolate as thin as possible, mix with the ras el hanout and divide over 4 spoons. Lay some salt crystals on the chocolate. Divide the mango puree and put in the centre of 4 plates. Place mango cubes and potato cookies on top. Spoon cream on the big slice of mango and put on top of the cookies. Serve with the spoons of spiced chocolate.

## Fried banana with cocoa

*For four people:* 50 g spiced-sugar water (see recipe), 4 organic bananas, 2 Tbs butter, 1 Tbs crystal sugar, 4 passion fruits, 150 g spiced sugar water, 2 threads of chili, 200 g lukewarm milk, 3 egg yolks, 2 Tbs cocoa powder, 1 dash of ras el hanout, chocolate ice cream.
*For the sugar water:* 200 g sugar, 400 g water, ½ a vanilla bean, 4 black pepper corns, 5 anise seeds. ¼ grated nutmeg, 2 cloves.
*For the spice mix:* 2 passion fruits, ¼ pomegranate, juice and peel of 1 lime, 1 Tbs dried lemon peel, 1 Tbs dried orange peel, lemon balm, mint, lemon thyme.

For the sugar water, heat all ingredients and simmer. Pass through a sieve and set aside to cool. For the spice mix, mix all ingredients and add 50 g of the prepared sugar water. Marinate in the fridge. For the cocoa foam, whip the milk and three egg yolks, cocoa powder and ras el hanout to create a fluffy sabayon. Peel the bananas, fry in butter and caramelize lightly in the crystal sugar. Add the flesh of the passion fruit and the chili threads and fry for 5-7 minutes. Place hot banana on a plate, sprinkle generously with the spice mix and serve with cocoa foam and chocolate ice cream.

# Bruges

## *Chocolate City*

**Although the whole kingdom is world famous for its chocolate, this city calls itself the Chocolate City of Belgium. Centuries old little houses give a warm feeling of friendliness; the imposing streets represent a convincing richness. The high and mighty towers show a glorious past. What can we discover in the field of pâtisserie in this Venice of the north?**

Sometimes it is hard to find your way around in Bruges with its labyrinth of narrow alleys and old little houses. Fortunately, the center is not large and you can find your way easily with a map. The real obstacles are the many tourists. Every five minutes, your path is cut off by a new group of tourists, clicking away with their fancy cameras. There are a lot of attractions for them in Bruges. Taking a tour on the canals, a ride with a horse carriage, a visit to the many churches, going into a lace shop... and of course the chocolate shops. With over 50 praline shops, it's easy to understand why Bruges is called the chocolate city. Most of these stores have their own workshops, often located outside the city, as the space behind the counters is too small for manufacturing. Unfortunately, it was impossible to visit all of the chocolatiers, but we did our best.

### Detavernier

We start off with Stefaan Detavernier. His shop of the same name is a feast for your eyes. This noble house built in 1624 has a store and a tearoom. Stefaan went to baking school and always had a tremendous passion for this profession. Very sadly he developed an allergy to flour, a nightmare for any baker or pâttisier. Starting a new career would be a waste of all his education and know-how. He decided to leave most of his practice work to his right hand man, Bart Fremaut. You will find at least twenty kinds of breads in his shop, with the twenty-grain bread as the jewel of the store. Of course the pralines, petit fours and cakes are also a big part of the business. Here, quality is the key. Stefaan: "My principle has always been to deliver quality. In butter cake you use real butter, right? As a baker or pâtissier you are a professional and should be proud of that. The ambition to deliver quality was hard at the start. I saw people queuing up at my neighbour for breads I would not be proud of. Fortunately, more and more natives of Bruges discovered my store and it turned the tide. The bakery that was my neighbour, no longer exists." We visit his workshop, where 30 people are employed. They work in shifts, night and day. They don't only produce for his own store; Detavernier also delivers to other bakeries and hotels. Bart has just started to work on the new summer Las Vegas Tart. We ask him to describe his style. Bart: "Our style is rather modern, not extreme, it is all about taste. We take a certain flavour as a base and look for flavours that go well with it. We pay a lot of attention to the building of tastes."

**www.tearoom-carpediem.be**

## Las Vegas

*For 2 large tarts:* one slice of almond biscuit, chocolate glazing. chocolate galettes, strawberries and gold leaves.
*Strawberry compôte:* 1500 g strawberries, 125 g lemon juice, 500 g raspberries, 525 g sugar, 75 g gelatin powder, 450 g water.
*Chocolate mousse:* 220 g paté à bombe. 260 g chocolate 65%, 530 g whipped cream.
*Citrus cream:* 1300 g milk, 2 vanilla beans, 500 g sugar, 150 g Cointreau, 700 g loose whipped cream, 50 g gelatin powder, 300 g water, zest of 3 oranges.

For the compôte, mix water and gelatin powder. Cook all the required ingredients to a compôte and then stir in the soaked gelatin. Pour this in a silicone mould and freeze. For the mousse, mix the paté à bombe with the chocolate and stir in the whipped cream. For the citrus cream, mix the water and gelatin powder. Boil the milk with the vanilla beans, sugar and Cointreau, dissolve the gelatin in it and let cool. As soon as the mixture starts to thicken, stir in the cream and finely chopped zest. Build the tart in layers. Start with the chocolate mousse, then a layer of biscuit and then the citrus cream. Press the compôte in the cream. Smooth the top of the tart and put in freezer. Glaze the frozen tart and garnish with galettes, strawberries and gold leaves.

## Confiserie

Between the antique stands at the village market we find Bob. He makes throat pastilles, pommes d'amour and flinkaarts the authentic way. This last candy is also called Brugge spek and is made from classic sugar syrup with brown sugar, molasses and almonds. Bob has been a standard fixture at the market for the last 33 years. After chatting with Bob, we move up the small alleys, in search of cute stores and specialties. At the Mariastraat we find Zucchero, a sour candy store. We had seen the same concept in Amsterdam, but in Belgium, Dries Cnockaert is the only artist with a similar store. Dries is an experienced pâtissier; many trips abroad to places such as Austria and Iceland provided him with even more pâtisserie knowledge. He got his sour candy experience in Australia and used that knowledge to launch a great success in Belgium. Next to Zucchero is Chocolaterie Depla, a beautiful shop with an impressive

window display. The owner is Pol Depla, who was working hard in his workshop when we visited. Not strange, because with 48 different kinds of pralines, there isn't much time to do anything else. Pol is famous for his truffles. Since 1957, Depla has been a phenomenon in Bruges. Why? Like many others, he uses the best ingredients to keep a high standard of quality. Depla is a family owned business with Pol as the second generation. The flavours are surprising, as they clearly differ form traditional flavours. Further down on Mariastraat we find "The Old Chocolate House". Barbe Van Den Houte, who runs the little shop with her mother, welcomes us. We don't just find pralines, but another abundance of delicacies as well. What about chocolate gin or liquor, different kinds of breakfast cakes, and beautiful enamel signs with chocolate as a theme? Every season, a large part of the praline collection changes.

## Cookies and Breasts

We are now arriving in the Wollestraat at "Juliette's Cookies Corner". As the name implies, it is a cookie shop. This shop, started in 2004 by Pieter and Elisabeth Mulier, is named after their daughter. Before this, they operated a big industrial chocolaterie. Elisabeth wanted something different, something more delicate. The most obvious idea would be to start a small chocolaterie, but she thought there are already so many to compete with. Pieter came up with the idea to start baking cookies and the people of Bruges showed a keen interest. The smell on the street of the freshly baked cookies lures the customers inside, including our editor and photographer. There we found twenty-five different kinds of cookies, an assortment of cookie jars and other cute cookie gadgets. The store is very proud of its Brugges kant (lace from Bruges), a Florentine so thin that it resembles lace. Inside, an employee named Katrien is busy baking in what is clearly a paradise for cookie lovers. Craft and perfection play the key role in these products. You will not find one gram of margarine in this bakery, only the best butter and the freshest eggs are used.

Kitty-corner to Juliette's we spie a very interesting form of chocolate. Chocolate breasts in several colours, but only one size! We guess it is a C cup. Whatever you might think, a large group of Japanese tourists is having a good laugh at this shop. We are curious and go inside to meet Grietje, the owner of "Het Chocolade Huisje" (the little chocolate house). "It has been here for over twenty years. In those days we didn't have as many chocolatiers as today. The idea of the breasts comes from the previous owner, who had even a patent on them. When we took the store over, we also took over the patent; it has been a great success." We think that large breasts are always successful; the love for plump round forms is in our genes.

It seems that each chocolatier in Bruges has his specialty. In addition to the many chocolate figurines and pralines, we also find a basket full of marzipan fruit. And you can get this delicacy the whole year, not just in the dark December days. Why does the pâtissier of Het Chocolade Huis make these labour intensive delicacies? "It is love for the profession," says Grietje. In the workshop Henk Deceukelier is at the helm, a consummate craftsman. He deserves all the credit, because he takes care of fresh good quality ingredients every day, and does this with a very small team. Too bad for us, because Grietje does not want to be photographed with the chocolate breasts! So we have to look for another volunteer...

223

## Brugse kant
lace of Bruges

*For a full cookie jar:* 750 g butter, 2750 g sugar, 50 g cinnamon powder, 25 g salt, 500 ml water, 1250 g flour, 750 g chopped almonds.

Melt the butter and mix it with the sugar, cinnamon, salt and water. Stir in the flour and carefully blend in the chopped almonds. Let the dough rest for several hours in the fridge. Form little balls with a spoon or ice cream scoop and put on parchment paper. Cover with plastic foil and flatten a bit. Take the foil off and bake cookies for 8 minutes in the oven at 180°C/350°F. If necessary you can still form the cookies after baking.

## Servaas Van Mullem

We are visiting another special pâtissier who is working with viennoiserie, we find him on the corner of the Vlamingstraat, right across from the opera building: Servaas Van Mullem. His pâtisserie-salon has a rich history, because it started with his grandfather and great grandfather. The story goes back to 1903 when brothers Ernest and Honoré Van Mullem start the business at exactly the same spot. Then Herman Van Mullem took the business over. Unfortunately for Herman, his son wanted to become an antiquair. "My grandfather always regretted that my father wasn't interested in the business. He was extremely happy, when he heard that I wanted to go in this profession. Sadly, he was not able to witness the opening of my store." The store with tearoom is

completely restored in the same old style wherever possible. After Herman, the shop became a clothing store, but fortunately the building stayed in the family. When the clothing store closed down, Servaas could start his business. The production is done in the cellar. In this small space, it is tough to get everything done. Expansion isn't allowed as most buildings in Bruges have heritage status. Servaas is not an old fashioned pâtissier, but we do not find wild creations here. "Because Van Mullem is a name that goes way back, the customers want the same taste as in the old days. For instance, I have a Merveilleux in my showcase, which my grandfather used to make and called it Yvonne. It is a simple pastry with meringue and whipped coffee cream and chocolate slivers." The chef doesn't mind that these classics are so successful: "The authentic pastries are commercially very interesting. Take Yvonne for example. Those are very easy to make with relatively cheap ingredients. If I come up with a new creation, it always has at least four different preparations. Although they might be more intriguing, they are a lot more work. It is important to find a good balance between classic and today's pâtisserie." Servaas is a late bloomer, because he started when he was in his thirties. He took a speed course at Ter Groene Poorte and worked at Del Rey and Mahieu. We notice that his prices are very low. "You won't find prices here that Pierre Hermé asks, Bruges is too small for that. Furthermore, I want my clients to be able to afford it." Really everything is made from scratch, from puff pastry to confitures, which they serve for breakfast. When we leave, we get the recipe for the Merveilleux.

## Merveilleux Yvonne

*For about 30 pastries:* 1 L egg white, 2 kg sugar, coffee, cream, sugar, chocolate slivers.

Beat egg whites with sugar au bain marie for 10 minutes, then beat the foam for 45 minutes cold. Pipe small rounds on a baking sheet and bake the meringue at 150ºC/300ºF for 60 minutes with no steam. Whip the cream and add sugar and coffee to taste. Pipe the cream between two rounds of meringue and mask the sides. Garnish with chocolate slivers.

## Yet more chocolate

We now have arrived at one of the highlights of our visit. No, not a choco-latier, pâtissier or baker, but a museum! For every chocolate lover, this is mandatory education. The chocolate museum, which is called Choco-Story, is an initiative of Eddy Van Belle. He had a career in pâtisserie ingredients and then chocolate. At that time he decided to create a small museum in his business, so that his employees could see how baking was practiced in the old days. When he traveled, he always brought some-thing back with him and his collection grew larger all the time. To give his extensive collection a nice place where everyone could enjoy it, he and Jacky Vergote started the present museum. Jacky is a chocolatier and is in charge of the technical part of the museum. We get a private tour with lots of enthusiasm. You can see a big smile on Eddy's face when he tells us all about the chocolate relics. We are allowed to look behind the scenes, where we find a number of Codexen, Mayan scripts, in which chocolate is described as the drink of the Gods. The museum is not a collection of dusty rooms with old junk. At Choco-Story, the story of chocolate is told in an enjoyable and educational way, starting with the Mayans to the present day. We find out almost everything we want to know about chocolate. At the end of the tour we meet Jacky again, who shows the public how the perfect pralines are made. Why is Bruges the chocolate city and not Antwerp or Brussels? Jacky: "Don't look for century-old history. When people in the world talk about chocolate, they always mention Belgium. The worldwide reputation of Belgium is enormous. The advantage of Bruges is the fact that millions of tourists visit here every year. If they want to take a souvenir home, they always take a box of delicious pralines. Because of that, Bruges got more and more chocolatiers, it enhanced the worldwide reputation, and it increased tourism. It is an upward spiral, that doesn't seem to stop."

**www.choco-story.be**

## Appropriate Confidence

That the people from Bruges are proud of their chocolate is logical.
This pride has resulted in the creation of the Guild of Bruges Chocolatiers. The objective of this Guild is the promotion of Bruges as a
chocolate city and to share the love and knowledge with each other and
the general public. The chocolatiers of Bruges are allowed to sell their
own Brugsche Swaentje, a praline with its own history. This delicacy was
created during a competition between the chocolatiers of Bruges.
Out of many participants they had three finalists. The final was held at
the market where three pralines were presented to two hundred and
seventy people from Bruges. The outcome was a surprise as the finalists
had almost the same number of votes. The three came together and
developed the Brugsche Swaentje. The praline is hand made and is filled
with almond praline, crunchy florentine (lace of Bruges) and gruut.
This is a mix of spices that was used to make beer in the middle ages.

227

# Dominique Persoone
# *Shock-o-latier*

One of the professionals in Belgium is Dominique Persoone from The Chocolate Line. In the shop window you will often find a beautiful showpiece, and inside everything is chocolate. In front of the shop window tourists look in to satisfy their curiosity. You will find traditional bonbons as well as experimental delicacies that just might go a little over the top. What do you think of snorting cocoa and a bonbon of little green peas and wasabi, or making bonbons with the help of a little marijuana pipe? For anyone who has an open mind for tasting and experimenting, we surely recommend these candies. Dominique has a deep passion for chocolates, which is obvious by his travels to South America in search of cocoa plantations. The photo albums and interesting stories he tells are proof of this. Once Dominique and his team have come up with a new creation, they go in search of the right chocolate. For this they use the Cyrano Box of Belcolade. This is a box with scents that come from the Origine chocolates, and therefore gives the best combinations. "If we have come up with an idea, the whole team starts testing for the best chocolate to go with it."

**www.dominiquepersoone.be**

### Cocoa snuffing

*Ingredients:* 25 g Real Dutch 24, 1 g neutral snuff tobacco,
0.5 menthol snuff tobacco.

Mix the ingredients. Draw a small line of cocoa and snuff it. The nicest
way to experience this is with a chocolate shooter.

### Praline with smoked cocoa

*Ingredients:* 250 g cocoa kernels, 5 g dried herbes de Provence,
3 g dried rosemary, 160 g Noir Collection Costa Rica 64,
200 g Lait Collection Costa Rica 38, 850 g hazelnut paste.

Fill a plastic bag with cocoa kernels. Fill a smoker with the dried herbs,
light it and fill the bag with the smoke. Try not to lose any smoke; seal the
bag and place in the fridge for 2 hours. This way the kernels are smoked
cold. Take the cocoa kernels out of the bag, grind to a powder, blend with
the hazelnut paste, add tempered milk and dark chocolate and mix well.
Line two cocoa forms with red Costa Rica milk chocolate and fill
with the smoked praline filling. Put both forms on a plate and place
them together.

## Olive oil praliné

*Ingredients:* **225 g olive oil (kitchen quality), 225 g extra virgin olive oil, 900 g Noir Collection Peru 64, 125 g olive powder.**

To make olive powder, dry some olives in a dehydrator at 55°C/130°F and grind them to a powder. Melt the chocolate, bring to the right temperature and mix with both the olive oils and the olive powder. Temper the chocolate until it binds lightly and pour on parchment paper on a baking sheet about 1 cm high. Let the chocolate harden. Spread the bottom with a thin layer of chocolate and use a wire cutter to create squares of 2 x 2 cm. Douse in tempered Peru chocolate and put on a transfer sheet.

## Bonbon of small peas and wasabi

*Ingredients:* **small frozen peas, pepper, salt, nutmeg, 400 g cream, 600 g white chocolate (Blanc intense) 500 g almond praliné, 200 g Lait Collection Venezuela 43, 60 g dried green wasabi peas, Noir Ecuador Collection 71.**

Line the bonbon form with Ecuador chocolate. Put peas through a colander, to get the juice of the peas and the pulp separately. Mix the pulp with the cream and heat it up slowly until done. Season with salt, pepper and nutmeg. Add the juice of the peas, cook thoroughly and pour this mixture on the white chocolate and blend until you have a smooth consistency. Line little bonbon forms with 2/3 of the cooled mixture. Grind the dried peas to a coarse powder, mix with the almond praliné and the milk chocolate; fill the little forms and cover with Ecuador chocolate.

### Praline with caramel of cabernet-sauvignon vinegar

*Ingredients:* 225 g glucose, 150 g sugar, 200 ml cabernet-sauvignon vinegar, 375 g butter, 600 g almond praline, 200 g Tabasco milk chocolate, 150 g nougatine made of pine nuts, Noir Collection Papua New Guinea 64.
*For the nougatine:* 30 g glucose, 200 g sugar, 80 g pine nuts.

### Choc-tail Tequila

*Ingredients:* 250 g Noir Collection Papua New Guinea 64, 250 g glucose, 250 g cream, 125 g butter, 2 limes, sea salt, chocolate balls, tequila.

Rinse the limes, grate a thin slice of the lime peel with a microplane rasp. Squeeze the juice out of the limes and heat together with the peel. Cook the cream, add the glucose and pour on the chocolate. Cut the butter in small pieces and combine with the mixture. Add the cooled limejuice and mix. Fill the chocolate shaped ball with the ganache using a cornet. Add some coarse sea salt. Fill a pipette with Tequila using a syringe and put in the ball.

Colour a ball shaped mould with cocoa butter and red colouring and line the form with Papua New Guinea 64. Caramelize the sugar with the glucose and deglaze with the vinegar; mix with pieces of butter and let cool. Make a nougatine with the required ingredients, grind this to little pieces and mix with the tempered milk chocolate. Fill the form with half of the caramel and the other half with the praline mix. Finish the top with the Noir Collection Papua Guinea 64.

### Italian Javanais

*Ingredients:* 60 g fresh basil, 1 kg Blanc Intense chocolate, 400 g cream, 80 g glucose, 50 g black olive paste, 2 x 500 g marzipan, 50 g chutney of sun dried tomatoes, tempered Noir Collection Costa Rica 64.

Cook the cream with the glucose, add basil and mix. Pour the mixture on the white chocolate and stir until everything is melted. Pour this ganache in a ganache frame of 6 mm high and let harden. Mix 500 g marzipan with the black olive paste and mix the other marzipan with the tomato chutney. Roll the olive marzipan and the tomato marzipan to 3 mm thickness. Put the basil ganache in between. Spread the Noir Collection Costa Rica 64 on the bottom and cut this in little squares of 2 x 2 cm and take these through the tempered Noir Collection Costa Rica 64.

*P09*

### *Comme Chez Soi*

*Ingredients:* 350 g sugar, 440 g cream, 50 g glucose,
500 g Lait Collection Venezuela 43, 4 g fleur de sel,
Noir Collection Ecuador 71.

Temper the Ecuador Chocolate and thinly spread the chocolate with a
pallet knife on transfer sheets. Let crystallize then cut into squares of
2 x 2 cm. Carefully remove the squares from the transfer sheets.
Caramelize the sugar and the glucose. Bring the cream to a boil and
deglaze this with the caramel. Add the sea salt and pour this mixture
over the little squares of the Venezuela milk chocolate. Spread out
smoothly and let harden in the fridge. Squeeze little balls of the ganache
between 2 squares of chocolate.

### *Your favorite soda bonbon*

*Ingredients:* 500 g Noir selection C501, 250 g cream,
50 g glucose, 500 ml coca cola, 200 g hazelnut praline,
100 g milk chocolate extra (M443) 60 g crackling sugar.

Reduce the coca cola to syrup. Bring cream to a boil, pour over the dark
chocolate, stir till smooth and add the syrup. Pour in a baking sheet and
let cool in the fridge. Combine the hazelnut praline with the tempered
chocolate and add the crackling sugar. Cover the ganache with the milk
chocolate and cut into little squares of 2 x 2 cm. Take them through the
tempered Noir selection.

### Cocagne

Regrettably, our visit comes to an end. We have made new friends and
tasted even more pralines. Bruges, a city of delicacies, relaxation,
a Cocagne. We recommend this city wholeheartedly to our readers.
Here, you can learn so much in one day. Take the same route as we did.
And finish your day, as we did, with dinner at Sans Cravate, the restaurant of the young chef Henk Van Oudenhove, where simplicity is paired
with a Michelin star. Class!

# The Cactus Fig

From the window of the plane we can see that Sicily is quite a special piece of Europe with a very different landscape. High above the rest of the land we can see the Mount Etna volcano actively spewing little clouds in the air. Next to this jet-black mass a green valley comes in sight, the Plana di Catania with its hundreds of thousands of orange trees. But further up we can hardly see anything green. After we have landed we get a rush of excitement, as we believe that we are the very first journalists who have decided to look for the cactus fig.

In our country the cactus is seen as a strange prickly thing that needs very little water. Near the small town of San Cono these cacti grow in abundance. The Spanish conquerors from South America brought this plant into Europe as a kind gesture. Columbus, who thought he had arrived in India, called this cactus fruit Fico d'Indai (Indian fig). Now it is called Ficodinda. We keep the logic and call it cactus fig. The cactus fig didn't come to Sicily for its gastronomic quality. For centuries the plant served as a prickly wire to keep goats and sheep inside the fence.

The cactus fig was also known as bread for the poor. People started to carefully cultivate them about thirty years ago. This was because many Sicilians went to work in northern Italy and asked the vegetable man for this fruit. 66,000 tonnes are grown in Italy every year of which 90 per cent are produced in Sicily, mostly in the area of San Cono. Around this little town 3000 hectares are planted with this fruit. Most of the residents are involved with this in one way or another. This typical plant can grow up to five metres high and can be seen everywhere. The plant proliferates easily; pick a leaf and put it in the ground in the spring.

## The cultivation

Once the seed of this plant starts to grow it takes three years to get the first crop. After that it delivers fruits forever as it can live for hundreds of years. They are pruned in early May so they don't grow too tall which would make harvesting quite difficult. They bloom at the end of May when the first fruits start to show. Since an early harvest does not provide good quality, all these fruits are destroyed. The best fruits are harvested in September and October. The flowers show more or less the end result: yellow flowers give yellow fruits and orange blossoms give red fruit. A mature plant yields 100 kilograms annually, but that differs from farmer to farmer. It is known that the pioneers in the region produce the biggest, more beautiful and flavourful fruits. Those are the farmers that export. Farmer Francesco Rindone tells us "the outside world is interested in perfect quality, so there are huge price differences." We see many black wires hanging in the field, which is part of the irrigation system. Juicy fruits need a lot of water and that is not easy to obtain in Sicily. Fortunately groundwater around San Cono is just 60 metres deep so it is easy to pump.

P09

## Senza spine

The family Spitale owns a cactus field of 87 hectares, one of the biggest farmlands. The driveway alone is 3 kilometres long, so we expect an enormous farm. Not so! The people are modest, the house is modest, and the buildings are moderate. We are surprised to see the kind of equipment they use. Once the cactus fruits are harvested they are put on a conveyer belt that separates the excess of sand and unripe fruits. After that the fruit is put in a smart brushing machine that removes the small prickles from the fruit. Once that has happened the fruit passes by a computerized system that sorts the fruits according to colour and size. The brothers Spitale have an important export-trump in hand that labels the boxes with senza spine, meaning without prickles. There is a selection of four standard measures. Extra means fruits between 150-200 grams, fiorine between 100 and 130 grams and seconda between 80 and 100 gram. Smaller fruits are worth nothing to the producers. However, this changed when a German wholesaler showed interest in mini-fruits and is willing to pay the highest price. This way the small fruits produce an extra income. For the rest of the exports (Italy is seen as the country of export) only the size extra is considered worthwhile. The cactus fruit is by nature available in three colours: red, orange and a white-yellow. The demand for red fruits is the largest. Sicilians prefer the orange colour.

During our visit we saw that many fruits do not meet the requirements and therefore are a waste. As a rational person from the North we think that we could find a little factory in Sicily somewhere that produces fruit juice or some basic ingredient for pâtisserie. What would you think of an ice cream, a fresh drink or a confiture? No, so most of the fruits are dumped, which doesn't mean there isn't any research going on. In normal cool temperatures the fruits can keep for two or three months. Sicilians would like to see the season extended. They are now doing tests with oxygen deprived cooling systems.

# Gold on the other side

**Sauternes has a catchy but expensive name. However, there are other kinds of wine in regions close by that are just as good as the medium Sauternes.**

Our story starts with a little stream "Le Ciron" that springs from the endless forests in Les Landes (the south of France). This little stream meandering through the forest becomes a small and deep river that usually stays freezing cold. In the Pyrenees another river springs: the Garonne. While this shallow slow moving river runs through the south of France the water becomes quite warm. The two rivers are joined at the village of Barsac, when the ice-cold water from one river and the warm water of the other are connected. In autumn this creates very heavy morning fog. Is this important in gastronomy? Definitely. The thick fog in the morning and the hot autumn sun in the afternoon create a special terroir. The mould Botrytis Cinerea thrives in these conditions and creates a dignified rotting of the grapes. The grapes shrink, and the juices evaporate, which gives a high concentration of sugar and flavour. The people who have benefitted the most from these conditions are the owners of Chateau d'Yquem. Because of a good marketing strategy, the Chateau and also every vineyard of Sauternes got worldwide recognition. However, the prices of Sauternes are astronomical, which is a good reason to look for alternatives and they are not difficult to find in this region.

## Directly Across

In the immediate environment where the morning fog comes in, several villages are part of the AOC Sauternes: Barsac, Sauternes, Bommes, Fargues and Preignac. The municipality of Barsac has also its own AOC Barsac, but that name is hardly used since the catchy name "Sauternes" will bring in a lot more Euros from the world market. Directly across the Garonne River, not even 100 metres away, the Botrytis is thriving just as much. So why don't we hear about Sainte-Croix-du-Mont, Loupiac and even less about Cadillac? AOC Sainte-Croix-du-Mont in particular should have a worldwide reputation. You can see Chateau d'Yquem from this lovely village. The unknown stature of these wines is rooted in recent history. Up to about 40 years ago, the farmers there produced only for the local cooperative and they sold the entire production "en vrac" (in bulk) to the wine merchants in Bordeaux. The pool of wine disappeared anonymously and the name Sainte-Croix-du-Mont meant nothing. Forty years ago the cooperative closed. In 1954, wine grower Roland Sessacq was the first to bottle his wine. His colleagues followed him later.

## Old Oysters

Sainte-Croix-du-Mont is a lovely little village that is built on a high
plateau. The little church, which still has remnants of the Roman times,
and the medieval castle are built on a ravine and look out over the
Sauternes valley.

The village seems asleep, but don't get fooled, because the 450-hectare
vineyard is farmed with tremendous care by 80 wine growers. It is
unique that the ravine on which Sainte-Croix was built consists totally
of old oyster shells. From the church square, via small stairs, you can see
the caves inside the hill where you can admire million year old fossils.
The oyster fossils also play a big part in the vineyard. You will find a lot
of lime in the hard clay ground and when they dig oyster shells come
to the surface.

## Monster Task

What exactly happens on the 450-hectare vineyard? Three kinds
of grapes are cultivated here: Semillon (85%), Sauvignon (12%)
and Muscadelle (3%). The vineyard is well taken care of, but it gets
interesting when the previously mentioned autumn mist comes

into sight. The botrytis mildew snuggles up on the grapes and does
its seemingly destroying task that is most appreciated. The grapes get
affected and shrink in the hot autumn sunshine. The harvest starts at the
end of September until the beginning of October and lasts 5 to 9 weeks.
The harvest repeats itself about six to eight times, whereby the most
mature grapes are selected and picked by hand. It is a monster task, this
long harvest, but the pressing of the grapes create a heavy, almost syrupy
juice with very high sugar content. The fermentation happens in small
volumes and is very slow, taking at least one month. The young wine will
not be ripe until at least the third year, either in tanks, or in oak barrels

243

*P09*

the highest point (118 metres) of the municipality. But not all grapevines are easy to reach: the 20 hectares of licoreux wines are divided over 22 large and small parcels, all within the borders of the municipality. The view from the chateau is breathtaking. Lousteau Vieil is an old family business that started four generations ago with farmer René Sessacq who bought a parcel for himself in 1845.

Martine, who plans to come again to Maastricht next year, let us taste several wines of different years, young licoreux as well as very old vintages. In the Cuvée tradition 1999 seems to be the year of tropical fruit and even coconut. The Cuvée Grains Nobles from the same year has dominant apricot, pineapple, peach, almond and plum flavours, which is obvious in the long aftertaste. Later, when we taste a 1976, it seems that the true freshness has not been lost. Only the deep colour gives away a certain age.

The vineyards of Lousteau Vieil are old on average, hundred years is no rarity. Although some growers talk vieilles vignes after 40 years, here it stays jeune!

## Little Angels

The average sugar content at Lousteau Vieil is about 12º. In real good years this can be 19º. In 2001 it became extreme: it even reached 23º that resulted in 8o of sugar remaining in the wine. Martine Sessacq: "The quality of 2001 is monumental, but the drawback is that the yield is relatively low. Little angels drank 30%!" She means that the little angels are the Botrytis. And what about bad years? Martine is very honest about that. The AOC rules allow adding 2o sugar. The small farmers would otherwise not survive. Watch carefully when you buy a bottle of licoreux and this is not just for Sainte-Croix. A quarter of the oak barrels are replaced yearly. More new wood is not necessary for this subtle wine with it slow yeasting process. Wood should never be dominant in a licoreux, should not even be present.

The life of a wine grower isn't easy even in Sainte-Croix-du-Mont. Although the specific terroir with its autumn mist can provide unique qualities, it can also have bad effects. There is a small butterfly or moth that can inject acid in a grape. Within 24 hours the whole vineyard can be attacked by aigre and turn sour.

Deciding when to harvest is always risky. Lots of rain can kill the botrytis. Depending on the weather forecast, sometimes the wine grower has to start the harvest before the grapes are totally infected with the botrytis. The sugar content and the quality are low then. More than a few wine growers have gone bankrupt because they made the wrong decision. Who is the one who can stay cool and calm, not panic and has a sixth sense? That is usually the best wine grower. The most famous Chateaux, like Du Pavillon, La Rame and Lousteau Vieil have these talents.

and this process has different sous-tirages in the first two years. Consequently it will be a licoreux (sweet) wine that reminds one of dried raisins, ripe apricots and peaches, and flowers like acacia and honeysuckle. A real Sainte-Croix-du-Mont still has a long way to go, because it could easily be stored for fifty, sixty or seventy years without losing its original fresh taste.

## Chateau Lousteau Vieil

As within each appellation, there is a lot of quality difference. One grower will keep the minimum requirements, another goes far beyond that. The yield of sweet wines can be 38 hectolitres/hectare. Some farmers are still doing the old pruning method that can give this high yield. Most of the growers are more concerned about the quality and therefore the yield is rarely higher than 24hl/ha, so very similar to the Sauternes. The wine estate we visit is one of the best within the appellation: Chateau Lousteau Vieil. We were already familiar with them because last year we met the lady of the castle, Martine Sessacq, who was visiting the Horeca tradeshow in Maastricht. The chateau is situated at

245

# Quarts de Chaume

On the outskirts of the Layon area, on the right bank of the small river, is a small vineyard where you will hardly see any bottles. Before you can get your hands on them the real wine connoisseurs will have snatched them up.

The vineyards of this appellation are situated on the foot of the hill in the municipality of Rochefort-sur-Loire. The ground below was formed well before dinosaurs were roaming around as the bottom was pushed up from Bretagne. The road to our host is flanked by chénin grapevines and is the only business that is allowed in this appellation. When we arrive we see Jo Pithon busy with a horde of American journalists. When they leave the French Elvis Presley approaches us. He wants to show us everything he says.

The vineyard is on land in the shape of a bowl, which protects the grapevines from the wind. The ocean is close by and wet and dry spells change regularly, which provides ideal soil for the pouriture noble, the grey mould. In the eleventh century, the small area of the Quarts de Chaume belonged to the monastery of Rochefort-sur-Loire. The fathers leased the ground to the local farmers and had the rights to one quarter of the harvest, hence the name. Jo Pithon walks with us through the vineyard, gives us a lesson in geography, and plays with his refracto-meter, a small kind of binocular you fill with a drop of grape juice. Since the dryness of the concentration (in this case sugar) is higher when the sunlight changes, this gadget can accurately read the sweetness of the grape. Depending on the ripening process of the grape, the weather forecast, the concentration of the botrytis mould and the refractometer, Jo will know exactly when to harvest. He lets us taste the mouldy grapes and they taste fantastic. He is happy with the quality of the grapes this year. Jo confides that he made bad wines between 1978 and 1990. He was tired of it and decided to make a drastic change to go for less profit. He stayed away from bad practices. Jo: "A wine grower who makes sweet wines takes enormous risks. One bad year can mean bankruptcy, which is why many growers are dishonest and add sugar."

## Development

The land holds 15 hectares. Outside the harvest season there are four steady employees. Pithon: "I plan to extend to 30 hectares, because it has happened a few times that I had to turn down an order of 30,000 bottles." How can he double the property on such a small appellation? That has to do with the redevelopment of the small area, Les Treilles, now underway. "We have become good clients of the notary. There were people who didn't even know that they owned a property."

The harvest of the forty-year-old grapevines happens in three or four stages, when the overripe grapes are picked within a period of eight days. The winegrower carries an enormous responsibility.

Jo: "Botrytis enhances the flavour. The ideal goal is to get it when the grapes are ripe. When a grape isn't ripe enough you get a concentration of nasty, green flavours." The selected grapes travel in crates to the pneumatic press, where they are slowly pressed. The fermentation with local yeasts takes place in oak barrels from the Bourgogne; this lasts until next July. Thereafter the grapes are ripened in tanks for another six months to get a balance and homogenous effect. When we taste the wines later the oak is very subtle. Our grower: "This is the reason why I get the barrels from the Bourgogne. When these are made they are heated longer at a lower temperature, which gives better and more refined aromas."

Jo has very old wines and gives us the opportunity to thoroughly enjoy them. As far as preservation: "A Quarts de Chaume can almost be kept indefinitely. If it does go bad, it will not happen in our lifetime." When he takes us again to another old barrel we notice that the concentration becomes higher. Our nose and mouth take us to a Maghreb full of dates and figs. The aftertaste is amazingly complex. The harmonic balance

between freshness and the high content of sugars is extremely pleasant. After the tasting of discreet and even secretive cuvées, like the Ambroise 1997, we have a dinner for the pickers. Anyone who has ever been part of the grape harvest knows that the meals are superb. Pickers, helpers and supervisors alike share their meals, an essential ingredient for the harmony in the group. There is a lot of laughter at the table, but the subject of conversation is of course the wine. Everyone has brought a bottle for blind tasting, and comments fly as the bottles are opened.

## Alternative

Not far from the parcels of Jo Pithon we find six hectares of Domaine Baumard, four and a half of which are planted in an interesting manner. The grapevines are very widely spaced and grow about two meters above the well-attended soil. Wine grower Florent Baumard has his own

principles. We can see that by the huge oak tree in the middle of the vineyard. Florent has been in love with this tree since he was a little child. His pruning methods have a reason: "A grapevine should be aloof but that already happens underground. Since I let all the foliage grow, the top leaves can do the work." In his business, supplied with an abundance of technical equipment, he is able to make the Quarts de Chaume less sweet and of higher quality. We consider Florent a defendant of the terroir.

The two vineyards we saw make different wines with their own characteristics. However, we don't want to be judgmental because a Quarts de Chaume is not a wine that you would drink at a sidewalk café. If you belong to the happy few who are used to drinking this kind of wine, you would drink it at a Christmas dinner, or other noteworthy special occasion.

# *Foret* Noir

*A German or Alsace Specialty?*

Vincent Kieffer is a pâtissier, who has a fantastic command of the regional classics in the Alsace village of Lapoutroie. The Alsace is part of France, but this wasn't always the case. Because of the many wars, this area was often either in German or French hands and that is why the locals speak half German and half French. This is also obvious in the culinary field. Take the Foret Noir for instance, which in Germany is called Schwarzwalder. But who cares as long as it tastes good!

*Ingredients:* a dacquoise bottom spread with raspberry confiture, sour cherries in their liquid, 300 g whipping cream, 30 g icing sugar, chocolate shavings and bigareaux.
*For the bavarois:* 200 g half and half cream, 2 egg yolks, 90 g crystal sugar, 5 sheets of gelatin, 70 g kirsch d'Alsace, 500 g lightly whipped cream.
*For the biscuit:* 16 egg yolks, 500 g sugar, 350 g pastry flour, ½ Tbs baking powder, 50 g cocoa powder, 100 g almond powder.

Make a biscuit of the required ingredients, let cool and cut in 3 slices. For the bavarois heat the cream on low heat until it starts to boil. Whisk egg yolks and sugar till fluffy, add the hot cream and prepare as an anglaise. Let cool and add the pre-soaked gelatin and kirsch. Spoon the whipped cream through the mixture. Use a baking form of 18 cm in diameter. Build the tart in small layers on top of the dacquoise bottom and finish with 3 layers of biscuit alternated with 2 layers of bavarois and the cherries. Freeze and take out of the form. Whip the cream really well and mix with the icing sugar. Cover the tart with the whipped cream, pipe small dots on top and garnish with chocolate shavings and bigareaux.

# europe

01. **Iceland**
   ◎ Reykjavik

02. **Norway**
   ◎ Oslo

03. **Sweden**
   ◎ Stockholm

04. **Finland**
   ◎ Helsinki

05. **Estonia**
   ◎ Tallinn

06. **Latvia**
   ◎ Riga

07. **Lithuania**
   ◎ Vilnius

08. **Ireland**
   ◎ Dublin

09. **United Kingdom**
   ◎ London

10. **Denmark**
   ◎ Copenhagen

11. **Belarus**
   ◎ Minsk

12. **Netherlands**
   ◎ Amsterdam

13. **Belgium**
   ◎ Brussels

14. **Luxembourg**
   ◎ Luxembourg City

15. **Germany**
   ◎ Berlin

16. **Poland**
   ◎ Warsaw

17. **Ukraine**
   ◎ Kiev

18. **Czechia**
   ◎ Prague

19. **Slovakia**
   ◎ Bratislava

20. **France**
   ◎ Paris

21. **Switzerland**
   ◎ Berne

22. **Austria**
   ◎ Vienna

23. **Hungary**
   ◎ Budapest

24. **Romania**
   ◎ Bucharest

25. **Slovenia**
   ◎ Ljubljana

26. **Croatia**
   ◎ Zagreb

27. **Bosnia**
   ◎ Sarajevo

28. **Serbia**
   ◎ Belgrade

29. **Bulgaria**
   ◎ Sofia

30. **Portugal**
   ◎ Lisbon

31. **Spain**
   ◎ Madrid

32. **Italy**
   ◎ Rome

33. **Macedonia**
   ◎ Skopje

34. **Albania**
   ◎ Tirana

35. **Greece**
   ◎ Athens

36. **Russia**
   ◎ Moscow

[ ◎ = capital ]

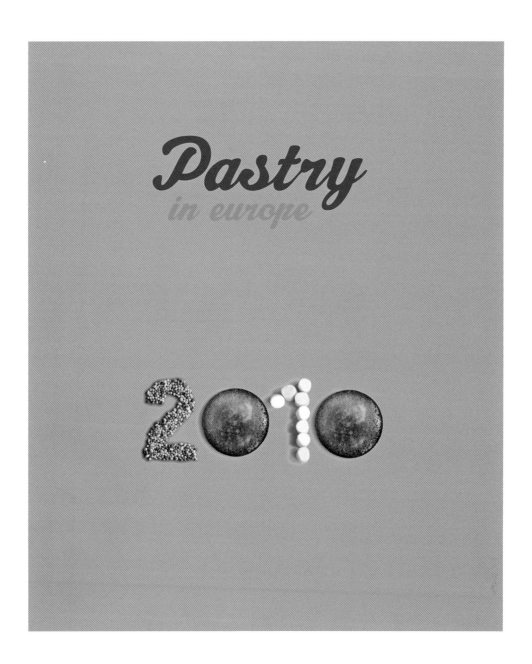

Available **december 2009**

*check our website*

**www.PastryInEurope.com**